COMMENTARIES ON THE SCOTTISH RITE DEGREES

I0407909

First Printing, February 2017

ISBN: 1542429714

Library of Congress Control Number: 2017900700

CreateSpace Independent Publishing Platform
North Charleston, South Carolina

For my father, Ronald.

My father always wanted to write a book and join Scottish Rite. Unfortunately, he was called from labor before doing either.

CONTENTS

LODGE OF PERFECTION

CHAPTER ROSE CROIX

COUNCIL OF KADOSH

CONSISTORY

APPENDICES

FORWARD

I wrote this book by accident; the result of taking an advanced study program, administered by the *House of the Temple* in Washington D.C. I loved doing research for the required essays, being thrilled to be writing about something interesting for the first time since graduate school. After watching the Knight Royal Axe degree performed for the first time, I realized it might be worthwhile to expand my growing collection of essays, notes and research into book form. This required far more work, but the Knight Royal Axe degree teaches us, *"If a job is worth doing, it's worth doing well."*

This book's organized to allow for reading individual chapters as desired, or, in a traditional cumulative manner. There's many long books already published on Freemasonry and Scottish Rite; many do little to kindle the interest of those not already involved in the craft, and, many are impossible to read just by subject interest and involve reading a lot of other material one may not have time for.

Pike's writing's typical of the era and contains what's considered grammatical and punctuation errors by modern standards, as well as very long sentences not typically used today. It shouldn't discourage contemporary readers and reflects his diligence as a journalist of that era; albeit with often complicated philosophical subject matter. A few degrees in the Lodge of Perfection aren't represented here; their rituals are brief and easy to understand from reading *Morals and Dogma* without guidance.

The ultimate motivation to write this book came from countless conversations with brethren in parking lots, and, friends interested in the Scottish Rite degrees. I've had many conversations with new members who had many questions; wishing I had something to give them to take home, and, which wasn't just another copy of *Morals and Dogma* from the long-winded Albert Pike, which doesn't always make for easy reading. I realized there weren't many instructive commentaries written about these degrees which offered discussion points; something which Pike did exceptionally well in *Morals and Dogma*. It's my sincere hope that the curious reader may learn more about these degrees, while the Scottish Rite Freemason may use it for reference, study and further discussion at lodge.

CHAPTER 1

COLORS, SYMBOLISM AND THE SECRET MASTER

The fourth degree, or Secret Master, begins introducing the new initiate to a vastly expanded symbolism than they previously experienced in their symbolic or "Blue" lodge. The use of color helps greatly throughout the course of the thirty-two degrees, with the multitude of teachings and symbolism contained in each one (making even the aprons & collars themselves) revealing several important clues about the meaning of the degree, and, it's practical application. As the introductory degree of the Lodge of Perfection, the candidate is taught the importance of secrecy, obedience and fidelity; they're also shown a small glimpse of (what they'll later discover to be the layout of the *Masonic Camp.* The royal secret, *equilibrium,* is built using colors to represent its several camps; the understanding of these colors begins with the fourth degree. Color and symbolism are inextricably linked in Masonry; the fourth degree begins awakening the initiate to the constant uses of allegory in the craft, utilizing both color and symbolism. "Symbolism explains the severity of laws and customs; to each color, to each pattern, appertained a religious or political idea; to change or alter it was a crime of apostasy or of rebellion." [1]

Further, symbolizing (with respect to colors) belongs to metaphor rather than to perception, and is thus a linguistic, and specifically rhetorical, not an immediately psychological function of the mind, which is one of the reasons why it has proven so difficult to establish anything like a "basic" universal system of color-symbols. [2] Freemasonry uses its degree rituals (particularly the "higher" degrees) to overcome the problem of varied conformity amongst different colors. The collar of the Secret Master in the southern jurisdiction of the United States, for example, is yellow, edged in black or deep blue. The yellow color symbolizes *light emerging from darkness*. Black (or deep blue) symbolizes the grief suffered by the brethren after learning of the murder of the Grand Architect Hiram Abif and the corresponding loss of the True Word. The importance of using a dark color to symbolize the grief and state of mourning which exists throughout the lodge after Hiram's death is highlighted by the dual use in the trim of the apron for this degree.

Black represents all but one of the Elu's in the *Masonic Camp* and reminds us to dedicate ourselves to the cause of freedom, to be generally liberal & tolerant, and, to be earnest, true and reliable. These lessons are reviewed in the ninth, tenth & eleventh-degrees respectively. Given the somber nature of these degrees, the color black also reminds us that it's a universal symbol of grief that's been used throughout civilization. It should be noted that violet has also been used as a symbol of mourning, but mostly in the Chinese culture. Fittingly, the third degree features a predominantly black lodge room.

Blue, we learn from the *Masonic Dictionary* is the symbol of perfection for the Hebrews, the symbol of truth for Druids, the symbol of Deity for the Chinese, and, a symbol of immortality to medieval Christians. The Blue Lodge introduces to the new Mason, the explanation that blue is the universal color of the fraternity, holding it as a symbol of perfection, truth, immortality and the Supreme Architect of the Universe. We know blue has been reserved for symbolizing divinity throughout history, with the Babylonians clothing their idols in blue, the Hindu god Vishnu being pictured as blue, and, various articles of Hebrew high priests clothing were blue. Accordingly, in the *Masonic Camp*, blue represents the first 3 degrees of the Blue Lodge. (The *Masonic Camp* will be discussed in detail in the final chapter) The first two degrees feature a predominantly Blue Lodge room. We also know that blue represents what's exalted and ethereal in nature, as it also represents *water, life, motherhood, eternity* and *the heavens*.

Yellow has always been considered as a symbol of light. The fraternity celebrates the light of truth by using yellow; this also represents the eternal search for "more light" by Masons. The *Masonic Camp* uses yellow for the banner of the twenty-first and twenty-second degrees in the pentagon, which teach that we should have faith in the power of Right, and, that "work is the mission of man." The twenty-second degree also reveals the motto, "*Time gives growth and strength to all things.*" Light emerging from darkness is both the fundamental symbolism and theme of the Blue Lodge experience.

Colors play a vital role in the symbolism of both Freemasonry and the appendant bodies attached to it, which begins with the fourth degree of Secret Master. The uses of colors, particularly in the *Masonic Camp* (which is revealed in a later degree) reflect the concepts of duality and the opposite nature of both the physical and spiritual world. The balance between opposites is at the fundamental foundation of the royal secret and thus the reason for this lesson to be spread out between the very first and very last degrees of Scottish Rite. The colors in the *Masonic Camp* teach us to always understand and appreciate the constant balance necessary to live a wise and virtuous life as a Freemason.

In conclusion, colors also help differentiate the various stages of work Scottish Rite members have performed in their search for additional light and truth. The caps worn in Scottish Rite uses colors to differentiate them from one another; the principal of turning the apron flap in different fashions to represent the degree of the wearer in the Blue Lodge is symbolized in Scottish Rite by the color of its caps, degree regalia and its lodge room decorations. The fourth degree a journey involving not only just symbolism and colors, but also one of interpreting both the obvious and the veiled forms of allegory, which the degrees' impressive imagery personifies. Finally, color also serves as a reminder of the overall values of the fraternity, which transcend country, language and religious preferences. An example of a fourth-degree lodge room from the nineteenth century is pictured on the following page; while it's in black and white due to its age, the overall examples of symbolism are easy to see.

For further reflection on the introductory degree of Scottish Rite, you may not realize that it was originally included with the three symbolic degrees of the Blue lodge; which all Master Masons receive. The purpose was to explain the colors and symbolism of the lodge that there wasn't enough room to discuss in the third degree of Master Mason. In the last century, the fourth degree has been removed completely from the symbolic lodge and only serves as the first of the Scottish Rite degrees instead. More detail about the reasoning for this development is provided in chapter eight.

SECRET MASTER.

A Fourth Degree Lodgeroom, Circa 1884 [3]

CHAPTER 2

INTERPRETING THE SIXTH DEGREE

This chapter examines the deeper purpose embodied in the Intendant of the Building degree, using Albert Pike's chapter on the third ineffable degree in *Morals and Dogma*. Pike summarizes the lessons in this degree in one convenient sentence, "You are especially taught in this Degree to be zealous and faithful; to be disinterested and benevolent; and to act the peacemaker, in case of dissensions, disputes, and quarrels among the brethren." [4] Pike also voices his strongest language (throughout all of *Morals and Dogma)* concerning the future application of the sixth degree by the candidate by stating, "Such are the lessons of this Degree. You have vowed to make them the rule, the law, and the guide of your life and conduct. If you do so, you will be entitled, because fitted, to advance in Masonry. If you do not, you have already gone too far." (Pike, 198) Pike clearly saw the continuity existing throughout Scottish Rite degrees (or the Lodge of Perfection at least) and, the importance of the candidate understanding both the lessons and the degrees meaning before moving on to the next degree. Pike's expressing also his desire for those who've received this degree to consider its practical application throughout the course of their everyday life. In other words, Pike feels the lessons in the ritual should not be left in the lodge room and should instead remain ever present in our daily lives. The chapter devoted to this degree in *Morals and Dogma* is uncharacteristically short for Pike and is barely six pages. It's a quick read and nearly every paragraph contains a quote of profound Masonic wisdom. The curious may even read this online for free in a relatively short period, especially if one is considering purchasing a printed copy of *Morals and Dogma* at some point.

Pike clearly felt that Freemasonry was a blueprint for a peaceful society; this theme is persistent in both the degree rituals and *Morals and Dogma*. He makes this most clear by stating, "…Masonry is the great Peace Society of the world wherever it exists, it struggles to prevent international difficulties and disputes; and to bind Republics, Kingdoms, and Empires together in one great band of peace and amity. It would not so often struggle in vain, if Masons knew their power and valued their oaths." (Pike, 197) In making this grand observation, he again returns to familiar words from the Blue Lodge. "See, therefore, that first controlling your own temper, and governing your own passions, you fit yourself to keep peace and harmony among other men, and especially the brethren. Above all remember that Masonry is the realm of peace, and that "among Masons there must be no dissension, but only that noble See, therefore, that first controlling your own temper, and governing your own passions, you fit yourself to keep peace and harmony among other men, and especially the brethren. Above all remember that Masonry is the realm of peace, and that "among Masons there must be no dissension, but only that noble *emulation, which can best work and best agree.*"" (Pike, 197)

Pike has a strong view about this subject, particularly with respect to disinterestedness. "It should be objection sufficient to exclude any man from the society of Masons, that he is not disinterested and generous, both in his acts, and in his opinions of men, and his constructions of their conduct." (Pike, 195) Pike further expounds on charity with respect to the workplace. "The generous man is not careful to return no more than he receives; but prefers that the balances upon the ledgers of benefits shall be in his favor. He who hath received pay in full for all the benefits and favors that he has conferred, is like a spendthrift who has consumed his whole estate, and laments over an empty exchequer. He who requites my favors with ingratitude adds to, instead of diminishing, my wealth; and he who cannot return a favor is equally poor, whether his inability arises from poverty of spirit, sordidness of soul, or pecuniary indigence." (Pike, 195) Finally, he summarizes these two points in the overall theme of the degree, "*Nor can any man any more be a Mason than he can be a gentleman, unless he is generous, liberal, and disinterested.*" (Pike, 195)

CHAPTER 3

PROVOST & JUDGE AND THE VEIL OF IGNORANCE

The primary subject of the seventh degree is *justice as fairness*. A Provost & Judge "is taught to act with justice, deliberate with impartiality and decide with equity." [5] In learning to let justice be the guide of all our actions, and, being just in judging others' motives,[6] we not only learn the "moral justice" lesson Pike intended, but also about social contract theory. Derived because of the original position in social contract theory, the principal of justice as fairness may predate the original working of the seventh degree in the Rite of Perfection in eighteenth century France, when the degree was titled "Irish Master" and the name changed to Provost and Judge when Albert Pike updated the ritual to teach the moral lesson of justice. While the concept of "justice as fairness" resonates with the core purposes of Freemasonry, the philosophical concept of a "veil of ignorance" closely mirrors the theme of the current seventh degree Scottish Rite ritual.

The "veil of ignorance" concept is a thought exercise presented by John Rawls in his book *A Theory of Justice*, in which every person is bound by a veil, which "insures impartiality of judgment, of all knowledge of one's personal characteristics, and, social and historical circumstances. One doesn't know of certain fundamental interests they have, plus general facts about psychology, economics, biology, and other social and natural sciences. All parties in the original position are presented with a list of the main conceptions of justice drawn from the tradition of social and political philosophy, and are assigned the task of choosing from among these alternatives the conception of justice that best advances their interests in establishing conditions that enable them to effectively pursue their final ends and fundamental interests." [7] This is the ideal method of dispensing impartial justice, as the "veil" helps prevent the judge from exercising bias, as that persons' future utility in life is not known at birth, or, before the moment they typically may be judged. One may grow to become righteous as a doctor, whilst another of the same may grow to be unrighteous and a criminal, for example.

Rawls argues the most rational choice in this "original" position is derived from two distinct principles of justice. The first principle guarantees the equal basic rights and liberties needed to secure the fundamental interests of free and equal citizens. The second principle provides fair equality of educational and employment opportunities enabling all to fairly compete for powers and prerogatives of office; and it secures for all a guaranteed minimum of the all-purpose means (including income and wealth) that individuals need to pursue their interests and to maintain their self-respect as free and equal persons. The "veil of ignorance" essentially becomes a grand levelling tool for ensuring an unbiased and "fair" outcome is guaranteed. The symbolism of the veil in masonic ritual serves to teach a similar lesson, which is reinforced later during the inquisition scene in the twenty-ninth-degree ritual of Scottish Knight of St. Andrew. We're reminded that the veil is not only a levelling device of equality in masonic ritual, but also symbolic of dispelling ignorance; especially when being removed from one's head to bring the wearer from darkness to light, not unlike "the age of the Renaissance lifting the veil of ignorance from the European world." [8] It's fitting that the veil exists both in masonic symbolism and social contract theory as emblematic of the removal of ignorance, and, the rule of impartiality. Pike reflects on the concept of justice as fairness in *Morals and Dogma*, "Every wrong done by one man to another, whether it affect his person, his property, his happiness, or his reputation, is an offense against the law of justice. The field of this Degree is therefore a wide and vast one; and Masonry seeks for the most impressive mode of enforcing the law of justice, and the most effectual means of preventing wrong and injustice." (Pike, 200)

Rawls explains further how the "veil of ignorance" is applied universally, "Among the essential features of the situation is that no one knows this place in society, this class position or social status, nor does anyone know his fortune in the distribution of natural assets inabilities, his intelligence, strength, and the like. I show even assume that the parties do not know their conceptions of the good for their special psychological propensities. The principles of justice are chosen behind a "veil of ignorance." This ensures that no person is advantaged (or disadvantaged) in the choice of principles by the outcome of natural chance or the contingency of social circumstances." [9] This is precisely how a Provost and Judge should both act and judge when considering the fate any accused persons. Whilst Rawls was not a Freemason and was an atheist, he still managed to identify the principal lesson of the seventh degree in his own work; by contemplating the problems relating to *justice as fairness.* Justice as fairness is at its core, the primary directive of distributive justice.

In practical application to the seventh-degree ritual, King Solomon appointed "seven judges in order that justice might be administered among the workmen on the Temple, giving them an opportunity to have their complaints heard and their disputes settled." [10] The intentional choosing of an odd number of judges ensures that no tie may ever occur, which is the model all democracies use for their courts and tribunals. While the US Constitution doesn't stipulate how many judges the Supreme Court shall have, for example, Congress last fixed this number in 1869 to nine. King Solomon was indeed wise to take great care in using an odd number of judges, and, his wisdom has been continued in modern times. The normative concept of using an odd number to decide an outcome with potential moral importance allows for symbolic logic to be used; the resulting empirical formulas one may derive illustrate how an odd number ensures nothing as unfair as a split decision need ever occur. This is important when contemplating issues of morality (or justice) as fairness, the fundamental theme of the seventh degree.

While Rawls is required reading in American grad school courses in economics, philosophy or political economy, most folks never contemplate the concept Rawls pioneered of "justice as fairness" and thus by extension, rational choice theory; which is also known as game theory, or social contract theory. While outside this chapters focus, Rawls "veil of ignorance" can also be expressed with empirical formulas that may predict individuals' decision making; to maximize their utility fully. This concept of "utility maximization" is widely used in both microeconomic modeling and ethical decision making, and, formed the basis for a great deal of John Stuart Mill's classic book *Utilitarianism*. John Stuart Mill and his work obviously predates Rawls; however, the concept of utilitarianism was pioneered by him and has been the source of inspiring utility maximization exercises, which lie at the core of rational choice theory. The seventh degree teaches that in maximizing the utility of our labors, we must always strive to *dispense justice fairly* and i*mpartially*, as life may so require of us at any moment.

FURTHER READING

1. Arrow, Kenneth. *Social Order and Individual Values.* Yale University Press. 1963.

2. Bentham, Jeremy. *An Introduction to the Principles of Morals and Legislation.* At Clarendon Press. 1823.

3. Gauthier, David. *Practical Reasoning: The Structure and Foundations of Prudential and Moral Arguments and Their Exemplification in Discourse.* At Clarendon Press. 1963.

4. Mill, John, Stuart. *Utilitarianism.* Longmans, Green and Company. 1879.

5. Rawls, John. Kelly, Erin (ed.) *Justice as Fairness: A Restatement.* Harvard University Press. 2001.

6. Rawls, John. *Political Liberalism: Expanded Edition.* Cambridge University Press. 2013.

7. Sen, Amartya. *Development as Freedom.* Knopf Doubleday Publishing Group. 2011.

8. Sidgwick, Henry. *The Methods of Ethics.* Macmillan And Co. 1884.

9. Walzer, Michael. *Spheres of Justice.* Basic Books Limited. 1983.

CHAPTER 4

INTENDANT OF THE BUILDING: THE FIFTH INEFFABLE DEGREE

Scottish Rite's eighth degree is titled Intendant of the Building (it is the fifth of the ineffable degrees in the Lodge of Perfection) and was also known as "Master in Israel" in earlier workings. The lesson of this degree is that, "benevolence and charity demand that we correct our own faults and those of others. That which a man knows dies with him; therefore, transmit your knowledge. Labour is honourable if done with *sobriety, temperance, punctuality* and *industry*." (Hutchens, 48) While benevolence and charity is the focus of the eighth degree, the number five serves a common theme in the symbolism of the ritual. We know five superintendents (one for each order of architecture) were appointed by King Solomon to supervise the continuation of the temples construction after Grand Master Hiram's untimely death; the degree ritual chronicles their installation. [11] This chapter explains the symbolism of the number five in the degree ritual, as well as the importance of Masonic charity.

The lodge in this degree has only five members, representing the five Grand Architects (temporarily appointed by King Solomon) after a time of mourning had passed and construction of the temple had resumed. The five officers are styled as the Master, Senior Warden, Junior Warden, Master of the Ceremonies and Captain of the Guard. These five officers represent the executive leadership of the temples construction effort; closely mirroring the executive team model of most large companies; with one manager for every division reporting to a CEO or President.

The table below illustrates how the five orders of architecture were integrated into the temples management and workforce, as well as listing their office and position in a Lodge of Intendents of the Building:

Master	*ADONIRAM*	East	*President, Board of Architects*
Sr. Warden	*JOABERT*	West	*Chief Artificer of Brass*
Jr. Warden	*STOLKIN*	South	*Chief Carpenter*
M.C.	*SELEC*	North	*Chief Stonemason*
Cpt. Guard	*GAREB*	North	*Chief Silver & Gold Engraver*

We learn from Pike that, "Step by step men must advance toward Perfection; and each Masonic Degree is meant to be one of those steps. Each is a development of a particular duty; and in the present you are taught charity and benevolence; to be to your brethren an example of virtue; to correct your own faults; and to endeavor to correct those of your brethren." (Pike, 207) Some elements of the Blue Lodge teaching of relief are then expounded upon further in comparison to the sixth degree, where Pike stays, "To go upon a brother's errand or to his relief, even barefoot and upon flinty ground; to remember him in your supplications to the Deity; to clasp him to your heart, and protect him against malice and evil-speaking; to uphold him when about to stumble and fall; and to give him prudent, honest, and friendly counsel, are duties plainly written upon the pages of God's great code of law, and first among the ordinances of Masonry." (Pike, 217) The teaching that we must help our brethren as an example of how all other men should also help their fellow-man in times of need seems to be Pike's theme throughout much of his writing on this degree. It's of his opinion that such charitable good and benevolence are necessary before achieving a peaceful society. This idea appears as relevant today as it was originally in the nineteenth century.

Pike elaborates once more on the concept of charity. "Charity is the great channel, it has been well said, through which God passes all His mercy upon mankind. For we receive absolution of our sins in proportion to our forgiving our brother. This is the rule of our hopes and the measure of our desire in this world; and on the day of death and judgment, the great sentence upon mankind shall be transacted according to our alms, which is the other part of charity. God himself is love; and every degree of charity that dwells in us is the participation of the Divine nature." (Pike, 290) Clearly, Pike saw a strong connection between charitable deeds and divinity, which mattered not if the provider (or beneficiary) was a Mason. It's this element of Pike's sixth degree teachings that's most valuable to impart to the youth orders, for their benefit and instruction as *DeMolay's* and *Job's Daughters*, for instance, so they may properly understand such lessons before reaching adulthood.

Reflecting on the structure of having five superintendents as Directors of the work, we can look back to 1871 and Pike's suggested application of the eighth degree, "A Masonic Lodge should resemble a bee-hive, in which all the members work together with ardour for the common good." In studying the investiture notes of the older version of the ritual (hosted online by the *University of Bradford*) it discusses the visual symbolism of the number five: "The battery of five, the five lights on the altar, the five steps, the five-pointed star, and the travel five times about the body of the Lodge, are all emblematical of the first five Chief Architects." After a discussion about the cordon being crimson to symbolize the zeal in which an Intendant of the Building should act when practicing benevolence or charity, we discover a powerful reminder of the Master Mason Blue Lodge degree: "The number five in this degree, my brother, has many allusions, some of which have already been explained to you; it is also to remind us of the *five points of fellowship*: that we are to go on a brother's errand or to his relief, even barefoot and upon flinty ground; to remember him in our supplications to the Deity; to clasp him to our heart and protect him against misfortune and slander; to uphold him when about to stumble and fall, and, to give him prudent, honest, and friendly counsel. Such are the duties you are especially to observe and to teach to others, for they are the first ordinances of Masonry."

The opening of the degree has the candidate hearing *five great strokes*, which symbolize the *five points of felicity*. They are then conducted five times around the temple, at which time their attention is directed towards the blazing star and it's five points. The points illustrate, "first, that in the construction of the *temple the five orders of architecture* were made use of. Second, to represent the *five points of felicity.* Third, *the five senses*, without which man is imperfect. *Fourth,* the *five lights of Masonry* and fifth, *the five zones of Masonry.*" After being questioned about what the *five points of felicity* are, the candidate then learns, "to walk, to intercede for, to pray, to love, and to assist your brethren, to be united with them in heart and mind." The *five points of fellowship* (originally presented in the Blue Lodge) develop a new parallel with the *five points of felicity* in the eighth-degree ritual. The candidate then remembers the melancholy of the murder of the Grand Master Hiram Abif, and, learns to walk by the *five points of exactness*, representing the "five solemn steps taken in advancing to the foot of the throne of the powerful King of Israel, where the obligation is taken in his presence." In closing the degree, the brethren are reminded to "think often of the *five points of felicity*" before the Master and Wardens each rap their gavel five times. The brethren then clap five, seven and fifteen times, to symbolize the lights in the lodge, and, the fifteen masters who found the body of the Grand Master Hiram Abif.

Pike considered the lessons of *benevolence* and *charity* so fundamental to being a Mason that it was of little utility to advance a candidate past the eighth degree if he didn't grasp (and practice) these tenets; if they weren't already doing so. Pike foreshadows this concept with the introductory text in chapter eight, which states: "In this Degree you have been taught the important lesson, that none are entitled to advance in the *Ancient and Accepted Scottish Rite*, who have not by study and application made themselves familiar with Masonic learning and jurisprudence. The Degrees of the Rite are not for those who are content with the mere work and ceremonies, and do not seek to explore the mines of wisdom that lie buried beneath the surface. You still advance toward the Light, toward that star, blazing in the distance, which is an emblem of the Divine Truth, given by God to the first men, and preserved amid all the vicissitudes of ages in the traditions and teachings of Masonry. How far you will advance depends upon yourself alone. Here, as everywhere in the world, Darkness struggles with Light, and clouds and shadows intervene between you and the Truth." While Pike was transitioning from the jurisprudence lesson in the seventh degree and into one of *benevolence* and *charity* in the eighth degree, his suggestion that one needs to continue towards the blazing star (which has five points) in regards to Masonic learning indicates his strong preference for the candidate to understand and apply the lessons of both the seventh and eighth degrees before continuing in the Lodge of Perfection.

The early (*University of Bradford* copy) ritual of this degree contains a lecture, summarizing the future implications for the Mason receiving it, that's equally suitable for concluding this chapter. "You are now, my brother, a student of the morality of Masonry, with which, we trust, you will become imbued, as for some time you will be exclusively occupied in its study. Step by step you must advance toward perfection in the moral code of Masonry: each Masonic degree is meant to be one of those steps: each is a development of a particular duty, and in the present one you are taught *charity* and *benevolence*. With these two virtues, man can best prepare for that future which he hopes for. The law of our being is love of life-this wonderful creation of God-and its interests and adornments, love of the world; not a low and sensual love, not love of wealth, fame, ease, power, and splendour, not low worldliness, but the love of earth as the garden on which the Creator has lavished such miracles of beauty – as the habitation of humanity – the dwelling-place of the wise, the good, the active, and the loving – the place for the exercise of the noblest passions, the loftiest virtues, and the tenderest sympathies : this is the charity or love we would teach in this degree, for God himself is love, and every degree of charity that dwells in us is the participation of the divine nature."

FURTHER READING

1. Grand Lodge of Iowa, *A.F & A.M. Grand Lodge Bulletin: Volumes 46-47.* 1945.

2. Morris, Brent, S. *Freemasonry in Context: History, Ritual, Controversy.* Lexington Books. 2004.

3. McClenechan, Charles, T. *The Book of the Ancient & Accepted Scottish Rite of Freemasonry.* 1884.

4. Waite, Arthur Edward. *Intendant of the Building.* Kessinger Publishing. 2006.

CHAPTER 5

RETRIBUTION, JUSTICE AND "THE VENGEANCE DEGREES"

The ninth, tenth and eleventh-degrees (in the Southern US Jurisdiction of the *A&ASR*) comprise "The Vengeance Degrees" because of their story; which tells of the later fate that awaited the assassins of Grand Master Hiram Abif in the third Blue Lodge degree of Master Mason. In applying the allegory and teachings of these three interrelated degrees, the concept of vengeance is often mistakenly confused with retribution; this chapter seeks to clarify any misconceptions which may exist concerning the original extent of justice amongst the Elu's who were under King Solomon's charge in the degree rituals.

At the root of all three of these degrees lies the punishment of the three assassins who confess (and are convicted) of the premeditated murder of the grand architect of King Solomon's Temple, which still lies under construction. The punishment itself is the principal action of justice, which occurs in the eleventh-degree and constitutes the concept of retributive justice; a concept of justice that considers a punishment that's proportionate to the crime. It's with this conception that the distinction between retribution and vengeance must be understood. "Unlike revenge, retribution is directed only at wrongs, has inherent limits, is not personal, involves no pleasure at the suffering of others, and, employs procedural standards." [12] In this sense, retribution can be seen (at least in the philosophical sense) as the equitable dispensing of justice; or in other words, that which doesn't punish the accused unnecessarily or unfairly.

The conception as its viewed today of the proverbial "punishment matching the crime" was prevalent in ancient Jewish culture, and was espoused in the *Law of Moses* (or the *Torah*) specifically in *Deuteronomy 19:17-21* [13] and in *Exodus 21:23-21:27*, [14] which included the punishments of "*life for life, eye for eye, tooth for tooth, hand for hand* and *foot for foot*.*"* This also resembles the even older *Code of Hammurabi*, which is thought to be the first system of justice seeking an equal punishment for the offense. In the instance of the murder of Grand Master Hiram Abif, the punishment of death was equal retribution. Whilst vengeance is a popular term for these degrees because a death of an innocent person had occurred, it is not vengeance that's dispensed by the Elu's, but rather retribution. Immanuel Kant argued in the nineteenth century in *Metaphysics of Morals* that retribution is the only just basis by which a court may punish others. "Judicial punishment can never be used merely as a means to promote some other good for the criminal himself or for civil society, but instead it must in all cases be imposed on him only on the ground that he has committed a crime." [15] Kant largely regards punishment as a matter of justice, and "it must be carried out by the state for the sake of the law, not for the sake of the criminal or the victim. He argues that if the guilty are not punished, justice is not done." [16] This largely constitutes the classical theory of retributive justice; that the punishment should be directly proportionate to the crimes offence.

Whilst retribution is justice dispensed by impartial means, vengeance is generally regarded as a personal response out of revenge, which may or may not be impartial, just or moral in its application. If the Elu's who sought the killers of the murdered Grand Master were to have killed them and not instead brought them to King Solomon upon their initial discovery, it would have constituted an act of vengeance. The three assassins were brought by the Elu's to be judged in the court of King Solomon, where they subsequently confessed their guilt. It is because of these actions that retributive justice was instead carried out in the conclusion of the eleventh-degree. In summary, retribution is just and follows the principles of Masonic law, but, only when properly applied; whereas vengeance most clearly isn't righteous under any just system of law. It could be argued that in a just society, vengeance is no more righteous than any of the offenses an accuser may claim to be rectifying against the accused; however heinous those claims may be.

While the passion of the individual (or group, as is best suited for the murder of the Grand Master) typically remains driven towards the *eye for eye, tooth for tooth"* mentality when a heinous crime occurs in modern times, it's important to consider the righteousness of impartiality. Not succumbing to the passion of the moment is critical to justice being fair and impartial; imagine that one of Hiram Abif's killers (amongst the group of three captured men) was innocent and merely had been standing near them when apprehended…perhaps offering them assistance upon finding them out in the desert. If you found three men badly needing food and water in the desert, would you ask them if they'd committed any crimes before rendering aid? Would you think to consider whether they were lost in the desert because of being fugitives on-the-run from justice? Probably not. The lesson of systemic impartiality is made serious with murder in these three degrees; even if we *know* somebody's guilty of a heinous crime, they must have just as equal a trial as an innocent person who's committed no crime.

FURTHER READING

1. Davies, W.W. *The Codes of Hammurabi and Moses.* Cosimo, Inc. 2010.

2. Gagarin, Michael and Cohen, David. *The Cambridge Companion to Ancient Greek Law.* Cambridge University Press. 2005.

3. Hadley, Michael, L. *The Spirtitual Roots of Restorative Justice.* SUNY Press. 2001.

4. Hammurabi, King. C.H.W. Johns (Translator) *The Oldest Code of Laws in the World.* City Lawbook Exchange Ltd. 2000.

5. Harper, Robert, Francis. *The Code of Hammurabi, King of Babylon: About 2250 B.C. Autographed Text, Transliteration, Translation, Glossary Index of Subjects, Lists of Proper Names, Signs, Numuerals, Corrections amd Erasures with Map Frontispiece and Photograph of Text.* The Lawbook Exchange, Ltd. 1904.

6. Irani, K.D. and Silver, Morris. *Social Justice in the Ancient World.* Greenwood Publishing Group. 1995.

7. Kant, Imanuel. Gregor, Mary, J (Translator) *The Metaphysics of Morals.* Cambridge University Press. 1991.

8. Roth, Martha, T. *Law Collections from Mesopotamia and Asia Minor.* Atlanta Scholars Press. 1995.

9. Pavlich, George. *Governing Paradoxes of Restorative Justice.* Routledge. 2013.

10. Sassoon, John. *Ancient Laws and Modern Problems: The Balance Between Justice and a Legal System.* Intellect Books. 2005.

11. Zehr, Howard. *The Little Book of Restorative Justice: Revised and Updated.* Skyhorse Publishing, Inc. 2015.

CHAPTER 6

LIBERTY AND TRIAL BY JURY

The very foundation of Freemasonry seeks to teach *equality, morality and truth* to all men who join the fraternity, that they may be a good and shining example for others who're not Masons to follow. The rule of law has generally embraced these principles in western democracies; the mechanism directly affecting liberty has been, by far, the concept of trial by jury. This chapter explores the foundations of trial by jury and the rule of law, and, its application to Masonic law and Freemasonry.

The concept of trial by jury was first advanced in the *Magna Carta Libertatum*, or *The Great Charter of the Liberties of England* in 1215. The purpose for this requirement was to keep the authority or monarchy from not being indifferent to liberty and the rule of law. The citizenry offer a far more "fair" trial than the influences of corruption, greed and tyranny. No law can be justly applied to a populace if it's not unilaterally enforced, regardless of the standing of the accused. The best law can do no good if a king, pope or potentate cannot be held to its standard with as equal standing as the poor. Whilst King John was the immediate focus of the *Magna Carta* as written in most historical texts, he was the second monarch to have their power limited historically; this precedent was set in 1100 by the *Charter of Liberties*, which placed some limits on King Henry I.

In 1687, William Penn published *The Excellent Privilege of Liberty and Property: Being the Birth-right of the Free-Born Subjects of England*, which contained the first copy of *Magna Carta* printed on

American soil. Penn's comments reflected Sir Edward Coke's, indicating a belief that *Magna Carta* was a fundamental law. [17] The colonists drew heavily on English law books, leading them to an anachronistic interpretation of the *Magna Carta*, believing it guaranteed trial by jury and *habeas corpus*. (Turner, 211) The *Magna Carta* is still in-use today for portions of the legal system in England and Wales. The US Supreme Court explicitly referenced Coke's analysis of *Magna Carta* as an antecedent of the Constitutions Sixth Amendment right to a speedy trial. A speedy trial must still contain a jury for important matters to be fair and impartial. All portions of Masonic law also have the requirement that a brother be fairly tried by his peers.

As the *United Grand Lodge* developed in England, it adopted the legal model the *Magna Carta* had already established in England for several centuries. The model used today in America for the balloting of new members, and, the passing or rejecting of administrative affairs leans very heavily on the concept of a plurality of peers deciding all matters. The easiest way to observe the development of *Magna Carta* into Masonic law, is reading Albert G. Mackey's book, *The Principles of Masonic Law*, most especially chapter three, which addresses Masonic trials. The essence of a jury trial is coupled with a secret ballot in Mackey's formula for a Masonic trial: "When the trial is concluded, the accused and accuser should retire, and the Master or presiding officer must then put the question of guilty or not guilty to the lodge. Of course, if there are several charges or specifications, the question must be taken on each separately. For the purposes of security and independence in the expression of opinion, it seems generally conceded, that this question should be decided by ballot; and the usage has also obtained, of requiring two-thirds of the votes given to be black, to secure a conviction. A white ball, of course, is equivalent to acquittal, and a black one to conviction." [18] Mackey stipulates next that, "Every member present is bound to vote, unless excused by unanimous consent." This allows for a brother who may wish to recuse himself from voting without simultaneously having a small number of the assembled brethren deciding an outcome; this assures that enough votes are cast to not allow bias to be a factor. This level of detail is mirrored in today's American jury system; prospective jurors who know the accused, or have a stake in the outcome of the case (for example) can be excused from participating.

Eliminating *bias, coercion, corruption, despotism* and *favoritism* are the principal aims of a trial by jury in the rule of law for democracies; it equally is used as an effective "check" or "balance" in the administration of Masonic law, the origins of which can be traced to the *Magna Carta* and *Charter of Liberties.*

FURTHER READING

1. Forsyth, William. *History of Trial by Jury*. James Cockcroft & Company. 1875.

2. Lesser, Maximus. *The Historical Development of the Jury System*. The Lawyers' Co-operative Publishing. 1894.

3. Levy, Leonard. *The Palladium of Justice: Origins of Trial by Jury*. I.R. Dee. 2000.

4. Oldham, James. *English Common Law in the Age of Mansfield*. University of North Carolina Press. 2005.

5. Oldham, James. *Trial by Jury: The Seventh Amendment and Anglo-American Special Juries*. NYU Press. 2006.

6. Penn, William. *The Excellent Privilege of Liberty and Property: Being the Birthright of the Freeborn Subjects of England*. The Lawbook Exchange, Ltd. 1897.

7. Spooner, Lysander. *An Essay on the Trial by Jury*. The Minerva Group, Inc. 2004.

8. Von Moschzisker, Robert. *Trial by Jury: A Brief Review of its Origin, Development and Merits and Practical Discussions on Actual Conduct of Jury Trials, Together with a Consideration of Constitutional Provisions and Other Cognate Subjects of Importance.* 1922.

CHAPTER 7

INTENDANTS NOT ADVANCED TO MASTER ARCHITECT

The ninth, tenth and eleventh-degrees (in the Southern US Jurisdiction of the *A&ASR*) take a "break" from the lessons applied in the eighth degree (and earlier degrees in the Lodge of Perfection) to dispense justice for the murder of the Grand Master Hiram Abif; the Master Architect of King Solomon's temple under construction. The twelfth degree of Master Architect tells the story of the chosen few Intendants of the Building who were picked to become Master Architects. This chapter discusses the brethren who did not become Master Architects and continued to toil in their craft; building the "symbolic" temple in which all members of Scottish Rite participate.

It's important to understand that in the example of this degree, the Master Architects were elevated because of their management ability, as well as their superior craftsmanship in their specialty area. These brethren represented the very best of the workers in their guild and as such decided, "who best could work" effectively, and so on. We know from reading the charge of the twelfth degree that this is the way an ideal republic should choose its leaders, as not everyone is needed to supervise the work, but those who do should represent the best-of-the-best, since the opposite is true of workmen; where most of the working brethren are needed. In another aspect of this degree, the Chief of the Architects (called *ravbanayim* in Hebrew) symbolizes the constitutional head or chief of a free government. It teaches us that no republican government can long endure when the people cease to select for their chief magistrates the best and wisest of their statesman. "When selecting other than the best, they permit factions to select for them the small, the low, the ignoble, and the obscure, and into such hands, for sordid interests, commit the country's. There is, after all, a "Divine Right" to govern, and it is vested in the ablest, wisest, and best of every nation." (De Hoyos, 288) After reflection, it becomes clear that this was the very rationale embodied in western democracy. With America's congressional approval ratings at an all-time low, a government shutdown because of financial mismanagement, and, heavy criticism from western democracies for spying both on it's on people and its allies, a good argument could be made that not enough Master Architects are serving in leadership positions in present day America.

The management of the workers is an important task, but it requires many years of work as a skilled craftsman in a specialty (or trade) before even the journeyman is bestowed the title of expert, or master in modern day building construction. If King Solomon's temple were rebuilt yet again, but in the present day, the same breakdown of Master Architects of each trade would be established; the names and trades have just changed and evolved over time. Instead of artificers in brass, we have designers, electricians, plumbers, etc. To build a Masonic temple worthy of a Lodge of Perfection, craftsmen who weren't managing the effort (as the minority of Master Architects) were also of the highest level of ethics, proficiency and skill. It's the duty of the Master Architect to ensure that the craftsmen produce excellent work that's plumb, and, on the square, as they themselves have toiled to perfect such similar labors.

What sorts of more recent construction projects have had Master

Architects leading the work? The most immediate answer is the Statue of Liberty in New York; a gift from France to America for assistance in their democratic revolution, which required much collaboration, labor and management to become the symbol of freedom and perfection it is today. The following excerpt is from Barry Moreno, a New York historian and author of an encyclopedia about the Statue published in 2000. "Liberty's sculptor, Frédéric-Auguste Bartholdi, was himself a Freemason, having just finished the *Alsace-Lorraine Lodge* in Paris in 1875. Liberty's own name, *Liberty Enlightening the World*, was probably derived from the Masonic idea of illumination and enlightenment. Several powerful Freemasons were members of the French Committee (particularly the celebrated historian Louis-Henri Martin). Not surprisingly, the Masons were just as influential on the American side. Nearly all the major figures raising funds for the pedestal were Masons, including the architect Richard Morris Hunt. The greatest moment for the Masons was indisputably the laying of the cornerstone for the statue and pedestal at Bedloe's Island, as Liberty Island was formerly known, in 1884. The ritualistic ceremony was presided over by the grand master of the New York State Lodge." [19]

Many suggest that Liberty may not have ever been completed if it were not for Freemasons; it's fitting that such an item of elegance was themed after the concept of equality for all, with a woman prominently featured at a time they could still not legally vote in the country. Lady Liberty could only have voted after the nineteenth amendment of the Constitution was ratified on August 18, 1920, whereas the statue itself was dedicated (with the assistance of Freemasons and the Grand Master of New York) on October 28, 1886. The necessary labor on both the

American and French sides was the product of many Master Architect's and Intendants of the Building. The general workforce was able and plentiful; Liberty would not have been completed without their labor, which was managed by the Master Architects. Just as a few Master Architects headed the design of Liberty, they too had advanced from demonstrating their skill in past projects. Accordingly, it's possible the construction of Liberty in-itself produced a few new Master Architects as well…upon completion.

CHAPTER 8

THE LOST WORD: PARSIMONY OF THE SYMBOLIC LODGE

The greatest tragedy in the American symbolic lodge is the omission of the truth concerning the Lost Word. Whilst one can argue a true student of Masonic philosophy might decide to join the Scottish Rite (in the pursuit of more light and truth) where they may learn of the Lost Words discovery in the thirteenth "Royal Arch" degree, it's also well-known how frustrating this apparent contradiction is to the loyal Mason, who's curious mind initially propelled him to join the esoteric mysteries of the fraternity. This chapter offers insight into the historical development of this issue in the American "Blue Lodge" and resolutions which honor the due form and tradition of the Masonic appendant bodies. This contradiction frustrates both new and old brethren of the symbolic lodge and inadvertently causes a disservice towards attracting new members to the Scottish and York Rites.

It's with great irony that this subject of division and ignorance also exposes the single largest degree connection between the Scottish Rite and York (or American) Rites of Freemasonry; the thirteenth Royal Arch of Solomon degree and the fourth Royal Arch Mason degrees both discuss a similar legend (and method) of the Lost Words recovery. Much evolution has occurred in this area in the current ritual since the nineteenth century. While the lost word is not communicated in the American third degree, it was largely transferred to the Royal Arch and predates the legend of Hiram Abif. Masonic historian George Oliver once noted that "I have before me an old French engraving of the Ground Work of the Master's Lodge, dated in 1740, containing the usual emblems and on the coffin, is the 'True Word' in Roman capitals. This would tend to prove that before the legend of Hiram Abiff was introduced into the Master's Degree, the True Word was communicated in the Master's Degree and not a Substitute Word." [20]

In Past Grand Master William F. Kuhn's paper on the same works, he notes that "It necessarily followed that when the legend of Hiram became a part of the Ritual of this degree, the "loss" of the "Word" followed, as the "loss" is a part of the Hiramic legend. But the "loss" without a "recovery" would be an absurdity; to complete the symbolism of Freemasonry, the "Word" must be recovered, hence the necessity for a Fourth Degree, the Royal Arch. In 1738, or earlier, the story of the loss of the Word and the new legend, the Royal Arch, were gradually introduced into the lodges, and when the division occurred in 1751, dividing the Freemasonry of England into the "Moderns" and "Ancients," the latter organized a Grand Lodge and adopted a Ritual of Four Degrees, the fourth being the Royal Arch." We know that when the two existing Grand Lodges merged to form (the present) *United Grand Lodge of England* in 1813, they held "ancient craft masonry" to consist of Entered Apprentice, Fellowcraft and Master Mason, together with the Holy Royal Arch. This formed the precedent of conferring a fourth degree in the symbolic lodge.

Kuhn states that, "The series of four degrees continued to be conferred under a lodge charter until about 1750, in America at least. The earliest history that we have of the Royal Arch in this country was in 1758, when it was conferred under a lodge charter in Philadelphia. It was introduced into New York about the same time by an English military lodge, in Massachusetts in 1869, where it was conferred by St. Andrew's Lodge. Since that time the Royal Arch Degree has remained secure in its superior place. Chapter and Royal Arch Chapter succeeded the term Royal Arch Lodge. The word Chapter took the place of Lodge in England, for the first time in April 29, 1768. The word Companion, used in the Chapter (in place of Brother) was first used in England in 1778. These terms, Chapter and Companion, were soon carried to America where they flourish as elements in the Capitulary system of degrees." While the Royal Arch continued to tell the tale of the Lost Word, the fourth degree began to be phased out of the Blue Lodge, meaning that to complete the understanding of the allegory and symbolism in the Master Mason degree, one needed to continue in the York or Scottish Rite bodies. Hence the problem exists today in Blue Lodge Freemasonry, which is arguably incomplete without the degree explaining the discovery of the Lost Word. The attentive and well-read Master Mason will soon discover this apparent paradox on their own, through reflection and study. The clue that further "light" is available in the appendant bodies is also not explained, exposed or otherwise disseminated to the new Master Mason. It's unfair to all brethren in the fraternity to expect that a Scottish or York Rite member will approach every new Master Mason with a petition for degrees, and, that a new brother not be given ample time to contemplate and reflect on everything they've been presented before taking on more esoteric studies.

The resolution of this issue rests most surely in conferring the fourth degree in the Blue Lodges, whereas a third-degree proficiency must then be satisfactorily completed before receiving it. In such jurisdictions, the Scottish Rite would begin with the fifth degree of Perfect Master, to mirror the tradition in the York Rite of only having a Past Master receive the degrees, except if they receive the degree of Perfect Master. This allows for the "good and true Mason" to be given the correct instruction concerning the discovery of the Lost Word as originally intended in the symbolic lodge.

The Discovery of the Lost Word

SOURCE: *Morals and Dogma,* **by Albert Pike**

A perennial frustration to the Masonic scholar is the apparent contradiction surrounding the Lost Word. This is also known as an *Occam's razor,* which is the principle that no more assumptions should be made about something than is necessary, being attributed to William Occam; a philosopher and Franciscan friar who advocated the doctrine of nominalism. It's of great concern to those who don't miss detail easily that this issue is not addressed in the three symbolic lodge degrees, and, it's not immediately obvious that the correct answer lies elsewhere…in another degree system of an appendant Masonic body.

FURTHER READING

1. Blitz, Jeffrey. *The Secret Legacy of Jesus: The Judaic Teachings that Passed from James the Just to the Founding Fathers.* Inner Traditions / Bear & Co. 2009.

2. Cryer, Neville, Barker. *The Royal Arch Journey.* Lewis Masonic. 2012.

3. Dove, John. *The Virginia Textbook of Royal Arch Masonry.* C.H. Wynne. 1853.

4. Egyptian Rite of Memphis. *Ritual of the A & A Egyptian Rite.* Рипол Классик.

5. Multiple Contributors. *Abstract of Laws for the Society of Royal Arch Masons.* A.L. 1786.

6. Jones, Bernard, E. *Freemasons' Book of the Royal Arch.* Chambers. 1957.

7. Sullivan, Robert. *The Royal Arch of Enoch: The Impact of Masonic Ritual, Philosophy and Symbolism.* Rocket Science Productions, LLC. 2012.

8. Topley, Henry, W. *The Craft and the Royal Arch.* Masonic Order. 1945.

9. Tudhope, George, V. *That Masonic Lost Word.* Health Research Books. 2006.

CHAPTER 9

THE LUSTRATION AND PERFECTION

The Lodge of Perfection concludes with the subject of perfection and self-reflection, both completing the symbolic lodge, and preparing the new Perfect Elu to properly enter the mysteries contained in the Chapter Rose Croix and the Council of Kadosh. The examination of the soul, universe and history of time immemorial are represented by the lustration, or baptism. The purification ritual of lustration (which is learned later in the twenty-ninth degree) is older than many religious traditions commonly using it today.

We know it was used as a purification ritual in the Jewish law (called the *Tvilah*) that also involves immersion in water and was called a "*mikvah*" in the Jewish Bible. "For example, Jews who (per the *Law of Moses*) became ritually defiled by contact with a corpse had to use the mikvah before being allowed to participate in the Holy Temple. Immersion is required for converts to Judaism as part of their conversion." [21] We also know that "immersion in the "*mikvah*" represents a change in status in regards to purification, restoration, and qualification for full religious participation in the life of the community, ensuring that the cleansed person will not impose uncleanness on property or its owners." [22] It did not become customary, however, to immerse converts to Judaism until after the *Babylonian Captivity*. [23] While purification of the soul and the concept of being reborn are attributed to the lustration, it also serves as a symbolic reminder of divinity, of the obligations taken as a Freemason, and, the legend of the third degree. It is also repeated in subsequent degrees, such as the

Scottish Knight of St. Andrew. The foundation for the lustration experience begins in the fourteenth degree, however, and its importance in symbolism explains why it's thus repeated, outside of the Perfect Elu degree and the Lodge of Perfection.

It's important to note that the lustration in Freemasonry is not intended as a symbol of any religion, but rather a reminder of the renewal and purification of the soul, which serves as a fitting preparatory activity before receiving wisdom concerning the divine and truth; this also explains why it's used in more than one Scottish Rite degree. Lustration also allows the participant to reflect on the introspection of past lives. Using it as a common experience amongst all brethren who are conferred the various degrees also ensures a consistent experience, regardless of the religious tradition observed by the candidate.

We know that lustration is defined generally as being from a Latin word meaning both *gashing* and *atonement*. "A religious rite practiced by the ancients, and performed before any act of devotion It consisted in washing the hands, and sometimes the whole body, in lustral or consecrated water. It was intended as a symbol of the internal purification of the heart. It was a ceremony preparatory to initiation in all the *Ancient Mysteries*. The ceremony is practiced with the same symbolic import in some of the advanced Degrees of Freemasonry. So strong was the idea of a connection between lustration and initiation, that in the low Latin of the Middle Ages lustrate meant to initiate." [24] We know that much of the content in the degrees of the Scottish Rite contains "ancient mysteries" and so it's thus fitting that the lustration is used to prepare the candidate for the remainder of the degrees after those in the Lodge of Perfection. Lustration also reinforces the central theme of the fourteenth-degree, that of striving to be true to ourselves and to God. While reflecting into ourselves, we find that the tetragrammaton is revealed in its true form in the jewel of this degree, after being properly explained in the preceding degree. The lustration and the open compass (in the jewel) also remind us that the world is vast, but that we must be true to ourselves and to God, whither so ever we shall be dispersed amongst the universe. Finally, the lustration prepares the candidate to receive the fourteenth-degree ring, which is a sign of the compact made to the fraternity with the same fidelity we might show to the divine. Using the *mikvah* is fitting for those about to receive a ring with a Hebrew letter inscribed on it that represents the name of divinity.

CHAPTER 10

KNIGHT OF THE EAST OR OF THE SWORD

The Chapter Rose Croix begins its mystical journey with the fifteenth-degree, which occurs after the destruction of the *First Temple* in 588 BCE and during the ensuing *Babylonian Captivity*. The rebuilding of the *Second Temple* has been stalled, after previously being approved by King Cyrus of Persia. The date for this is thought to have been between 538 and 520 BCE. [25] Zerubbabel, the Governor of the province of Judah, travels to King Cyrus' throne and requests and audience with him; in the hope of negotiating his approval to continue rebuilding the *Second Temple*. The purpose of this chapter is both to highlight the importance of the fifteenth-degree, and, to explain the lesson imparted from the degree ritual. The symbolism of this degree will also be explained, with attention paid to the green cordon and gloves, the white sash worn around the waist containing the letters "L.D.P." and, the triple triangular jewel, with dual crossed swords pointing upwards.

The fifteenth-degree begins the four Chapter Rose Croix degrees, which are historical and philosophical in nature, being heavily veiled in religious allegorical symbolism. Consider the following passage on this matter. "The fifteenth and sixteenth degrees, of the *A&ASR*, are called Historical Degrees, for want of a more appropriate designation. They are founded upon historical events; but they are not historical in the sense of being erected to teach history, because they do not follow the known facts of history as all students know, or may know by making the effort. We must follow the practice taught in the Symbolic and

Ineffable degrees if we would learn the lessons sought to be presented by remembering that, "Masonry is a course in ancient, hieroglyphic, moral instruction, taught agreeably to ancient usage by types, emblems and allegorical figures." Only as we study these degrees as allegories shall we be able to gain any further Light in Masonry…" [26] Thus, the events presented in the fifteenth-degree concerning Zerubbabel and the rebuilding of the *Second Temple* are based on historical events and figures, but may not have occurred, etc.

Pike most eloquently states that, "This degree, like all others in Masonry, is symbolical. Based upon historical truth and authentic tradition, it is still an allegory. The leading lesson of this Degree is Fidelity to obligation, and Constancy and Perseverance under difficulties and discouragement." (Pike, 309) The lesson of maintaining fidelity to one's obligations under any circumstances is both the principal lesson and driving force behind the degree ritual. Maintaining our obligations (and silence for that which has been entrusted to us in confidence to keep secret) is a basic tenet of Freemasonry; as such, it's recommended that the fifteenth-degree be included amongst the seven fundamental degrees of Freemasonry, as depicted in Appendix IV.

Zerubbabel is begrudgingly granted an audience with King Cyrus by his guards and the king recognizes him instantly as having previously fought by his side. King Cyrus enquires as to the purpose of his travels and is reminded by Zerubbabel that his previous promise to rebuild the Temple had not been carried out, being instead forgotten. Upon being reminded of his broken promise, King Cyrus also remembers that Zerubbabel is an adept in the *Mysteries*, holding secret knowledge that even as a king, he did not possess, making him most curious. King

Cyrus then offers Zerubbabel immense amounts of treasure, as well as financing the entire reconstruction of the *Second Temple*, if he will impart this secret knowledge and wisdom upon him. It's at this point in the degree ritual that is the most important for understanding the purpose for its existence in Freemasonry.

Zerubbabel presents a compelling narrative to King Cyrus in his response. "…The honors and the rank that are earned by violation of vows are worthless. My life is always at my country's service, but even to free my people and rebuild the *House of the Lord,* I cannot sacrifice my honor. I keep the Holy Fire." (De Hoyos, 400) King Cyrus then acknowledges his mistakes and reveals a dream to Zerubbabel, that he'd experienced the previous evening, which carries with it a transcription of the symbolism of the green attire worn during the degree. "Long ago I resolved to set the Hebrews free, whom we've held in captivity for so many years. They, like us, worship one God. Other matters of serious import caused me to forget them, but I have been reminded of my duty. Last night I dreamed that I saw a lion ready to spring upon and devour me. I endeavored to escape by flight, but my feet refused to obey. Then, I saw Nebuchadnezzar and Belshazzar, the kings of Babylon, prostrate and loaded with chains. Above them, in a bright glory, was the name of Jehovah, God of the Hebrews. From the glory and the luminous clouds around it flew an eagle, saying that I should restore the captives to their liberty, or my crown should pass into the hands of strangers. Then, amazed in terror, I awoke." (De Hoyos, 401)

Zerubbabel then responds to the king about the true nature of his dream and his responsibility to the Israelites as a just ruler. "…The voice that you heard in your dreams was that of Jehovah, who, through his prophets, foretold your coming and gave you dominion of the east. The captives are the children of Israel who have now been seventy years in slavery. Their God commands you to restore them to their homes, return them their holy vessels, and aid them in rebuilding their city and His Holy House. The chains upon the kings betoken your fate, if you disobey His commands. And the lion represents His anger, which will swiftly destroy you, if you remain deaf to His voice." (De Hoyos, 401) The freeing of captive persons not guilty of a crime and persecuted merely for their religious preference is an entirely appropriate Masonic obligation and a continuing example of how Freemasonry does not seek to favor (or necessarily impart) any religions tradition over another; preferring instead to use symbolism and teachings from all religious traditions as appropriate; most especially in cases of moral lessons which are universally applicable to all religious traditions. The lion, traditionally a symbol used in Christianity (such as the one identifying Mark the Evangelist, or, the story in the *Book of Daniel* about his miraculous recovery from a lion attack, for example) is used in this instance for two simple reasons. The lion is known symbolically as the emblem of the *Tribe of Judah*, which eventually became the Kingdom of Judah. [27] Secondly, Zerubbabel was himself the Governor of the Province of Judah and the grandson of King Jeconiah, which is discussed somewhat in *Haggai 1:1* in the *Hebrew Bible*. [28]

King Cyrus then responds to Zerubbabel's interpretation and request, after commending him on his fidelity. "I will obey. Zerubbabel, I give you permission to rebuild your Temple. I do decree that every captive of Judea and Israel in my dominions be liberated from this moment...Bring forth the vessels of the *House of Jehovah* and deliver them to whomever you shall appoint. Let the House be built, and the foundations thereof be strongly laid, and the expenses be given out of our treasury. Let the golden and silver vessels be restored and brought again to the Temple at Jerusalem. Zerubbabel, you are the Governor of Judea. I order that you be obeyed in every place through which you may pass, and that all supplies and assistance be furnished you, as they would myself. ...This signet is the evidence of your authority and command over your people, as my representative. Exercise wisely and generously your great powers, always remembering that the prosperity and happiness of the people should be the constant care of a ruler; and that justice and equity and clemency are the fit supports of the throne. As a mark of my esteem, I also invest you with this collar, which you wear as a noble of Media and Persia. It is the decoration of an Order of Brotherhood conferred only on the princes of Persia, and as a high mark of honor." (De Hoyos, 402)

The first chapter of the *Book of Ezra* in the *Hebrew Bible* contains several references to King Cyrus and the events discussed in the fifteenth-degree. The following passage represents perhaps the best example. "In the first year of King Cyrus, the king issued a decree: Concerning the house of God at Jerusalem, let the temple, the place where sacrifices are offered, be rebuilt and let its foundations be retained, its height being 60 cubits and its width 60 cubits; with three layers of huge stones and one layer of timbers. And let the cost be paid from the royal treasury. Also, let the gold and silver utensils of the house of God, which Nebuchadnezzar took from the temple in Jerusalem and brought to Babylon, be returned and brought to their places in the temple in Jerusalem; and you shall put them in the house of God." [29]

Despite his stature as a prominent king and military leader, King Cyrus is only mentioned in one other book of the *Hebrew Bible*, which is the *Book of Chronicles.* It's no surprise that while the purpose of the passage is to show his acknowledgment of having God's permission to conquer the known world, it still mentions the rebuilding of the *Second Temple.* "Thus says Cyrus king of Persia, The LORD, the God of heaven, has given me all the kingdoms of the earth, and He has appointed me to build Him a house in Jerusalem, which is in Judah. Whoever there is among you of all His people, May the LORD his God be with him, and let him go up!" [30]

The green cordon and gloves symbolize the fidelity and honor displayed by Zerubbabel in the fifteenth-degree. Green also symbolizes the immortality of the human soul and Masonry. (Hutchens, 111) "As the color of hope, longevity and immortality…Green light plays a role among alchemists and occultists; it is encountered in nature during the rising and setting of the sun, where it appears as an extremely rarely observed manifestation of light known as the green ray, and, is a symbol of illumination as well as a symbol of death and life. The alchemists also saw the so-called secret fire, the living spirit, in the image of a green, translucent and fusible crystal." [31] The "Holy Fire" that Zerubbabel maintains with his fidelity is congruent with the green cordon and gloves worn during the degree ritual.

Morals & Dogma Illustration, 1871

The white sash worn around the waist contains the letters "L.D.P" and are initials derived from Latin, which mean *Liberté de pensér*, or in English, to weigh or consider. This sash and initials are emblematic of liberty, which Pike considered the main theme of the fifteenth-degree, despite writing only a 4-page lecture in the ritual. The triple triangular jewel, with dual crossed swords pointing upwards, symbolizes *liberty, equality* and *fraternity;* and, *law, order* and *subordination*. The dual crossed swords themselves represent truth and justice. (Hutchens, 111)

The rebuilding of the *Second Temple* (for the continuation of the Jewish religion and community as effectively conquered peoples) is the principal issue for which Zerubbabel's efforts are realized in the fifteenth-degree. The important lesson of liberty and what it means is paramount to the importance of this degree. "Liberty is rarely appreciated until it is lost. Most natural gifts are held in light esteem. Only those things that we gain through achievement are accounted worthy. Only those things which we have enjoyed are missed when we are deprived of them. Freedom is only attained by the man who is constantly upon his guard while he works. Freedom is only recovered—the lesson in this degree—while he is in the attitude of defense while striving to build character. If character building did not require effort, there would be no virtue in accomplishment. It is only that which we pay the price that we account worthy in our journey through life.

"…Masonry being a course of moral instruction, and nothing more, or less, it is intended exclusively—for the development of individual moral character…Working with the Sword in one hand and the Trowel in the other means living on the defensive towards our destructive emotions and passions, and, at the same time, giving part of our effort to construction of character as well." (Russell, 90) The legend of the Mason working symbolically with both a sword and trowel explains the original naming of this degree, which has since been shortened to simply "Knight of the East" in most jurisdictions.

The *Hebrew Bible* contains the *Book of Nehemiah* and *Book of Ezra*, which tell the story of Nehemiah rebuilding the various walls in Jerusalem; after first securing permission from the Persian court. While the mostly first-person narrative is concerned with the walls used to protect the city, the identical parallel exists with both the rebuilding of what became the *Second Temple*, and, the story in this degree about Zerubbabel securing permission from King Cyrus to do the same.

"And I looked, and rose-up, and said unto the nobles, and to the rulers, and to the rest of the people, be not afraid of them: remember the Lord, which is great and terrible, and fight for your brethren. And it came to pass from that time forth, that the half of my servants wrought in the work, and the other half of them held both the spears, the shields, and the bows, and the habergeons; and the rulers were behind all the house of Judah. They which builded on the wall, and they that bare burdens, with those that laded, *everyone with one of his hands wrought in the work, and with the other hand held a weapon. For the builders, everyone had his sword girded by his side, and so builded.* And he that sounded the trumpet was by me. And I said unto the nobles, and to the rulers, and to the rest of the people, the work is great and large, and we are separated upon the wall, one far from another. In what place, therefore ye hear the trumpet sound, resort ye thither unto us: our God shall fight for us." [32]

The original name of Knight of the East or Sword has also been known as Knight of the East, of the Sword, or of the Eagle, and, Knight of the Sword, as well as Knight of the East. The sword allegory concerning the workmen of the *Second Temple* is also mentioned briefly in the *Hebrew Bible*, as described above. The Knight of the Eagle is based on the symbolic meaning of the eagle in this degree, for liberty. (Hutchens, 112) Pike states in *Morals and Dogma* that, "Masonry is engaged in her crusade, against *ignorance, intolerance, fanaticism, superstition, uncharitableness* and *error*... let us remember that the only question for us to ask, as true men and Masons, is what does duty require; and not what will be the result of our reward if we do our duty. Work on, with the Sword in one hand, and the Trowel in the other." (Pike, 239) Regardless of the name used, the fifteenth-degree lesson and theme remain unchanged; that being simply that *fidelity and good moral character,* practiced by the individual, leads to liberty for society.

54

CHAPTER 11

PRINCE OF JERUSALEM

The sixteenth-degree of Prince of Jerusalem is the sixth fundamental degree of Freemasonry (see Appendix IV for the complete list) and continues the theme introduced in the fifteenth-degree; the building of the *Second Temple* has again become delayed. While Governor Zerubbabel secured the funds and permission to rebuild the Temple from King Cyrus in the previous degree, King Cambyses succeeded him and was indifferent to the exiles. King Darius takes power next and in 520 BCE the *Book of Ezra* informs us that Haggai and Zechariah rallied the people, which inspired Governor Zerubbabel to again seek assistance and support from the King. [33] The duties of a Prince of Jerusalem are to judge equitably and fairly, to act as the peacemaker, to provide aid of any kind to other Princes of Jerusalem, to keep faith in the beneficence and justice of God, and to press forward with hope for the oppressed and persecuted. (Hutchens, 122) This chapter expands upon the degrees lessons of *equity* and *justice* and it's symbolism.

After meeting with King Darius and informing him of the events which occurred in the fifteenth-degree, Zerubbabel receives the following response: "This then, is the Governor of Judah! Princes of Media and Persia, because Cyrus the King so decreed, this Zerubbabel whom he made Governor, laid the foundation of the *House of their God*, but it is not yet finished. Let a search be made in the *House of the Rolls*, where the archives are kept, so that I may confirm his command and order the completion of the Temple of the God of the Hebrews. Meanwhile ask what you will, Zerubbabel, and I will give it to you, because you are found wisest; and shall sit next to me, and be called the man whom the King delighted to honor, and Prince of Judah. Ask also what you will for your companions, and it shall be granted, and they and you shall be enrolled among the princes of our household…" (De Hoyos, 418)

The search is made in the *House of the Rolls* and Zerubbabel is once again rewarded and given permission to rebuild the Temple. King Darius has confirmed the decree of Cyrus and ordered the rebuilding of the city and *House of the Lord*. He was pleased to continue as Governor of the country on this side of the river. He also declared Judah to be no longer a tributary province, but a part of the kingdom of Media and Persia: and the princes my companions, as such others as I may appoint, to be princes of his realm. He also permitted our people in his realm who desired it, to return here with the holy vessels for the Temple, and has ordered moneys to be given from the royal treasury for the expenses of the building. Then he sent us, with safe escort, to the borders of Judah. We have thus returned, to rebuild the *Holy House of the Temple*; and the people met us without the city, and brought us here with songs of praise and doing us great honor." (De Hoyos, 419)

We learn later in the degree that the middle of the apron is (not surprisingly) a representation of the *Second Temple*. The sword and belt are emblems of a knight's profession, with the square and compass serving as reminders of Masonic character. Further, it's learned that, "The two ancient Hebrew or Samaritan letters on the apron are *teth* and *alef*, initials of the names of the two months, *Tebeth* and *Adar*.

The Israelites re-entered into Jerusalem, after their captivity in Babylon, on the twentieth day of *Tebeth*, the tenth month of the year. Their thanksgiving, after the completion of the *Second Temple*, was on the twentieth day of *Adar*, the twelfth month of the sixth year of the reign of Darius. On the fourteenth day of the following month, the Passover was celebrated. Masons in this and the higher degrees wear the apron in order that they may never forget that they attained their high rank and dignity by means of Masonic labor alone. Remembering their first estate, they may be courteous and kind, as well as just, to the Brethren of the lower degrees." (De Hoyos, 421)

Pike understood well that even in the nineteenth century, the precedent of symbolism as a substitute for physical activities had long been in order. "We no longer expect to rebuild the Temple at Jerusalem. To us it has become but a symbol. To us the whole world is God's Temple, as is every upright heart." (Pike, 313) This somber instruction begins this degree's chapter in *Morals and Dogma* and serves yet another reminder that symbolism in Masonry is often veiled in allegory. Given that rebuilding the Temple seems to be a difficult, if not impossible task in its original location, it's instructive to consider the other elements of this degree, which have been retired and exist now in symbolism only. "The Princes of Jerusalem no longer sit as magistrates to judge between the people; nor is their number limited to five. But their duties remain substantially the same, and their insignia and symbols retain their old significance. *Justice* and *Equity* are still their characteristics. To reconcile disputes and heal dissensions, to restore amity and peace, to soothe dislikes and soften prejudices, are their peculiar duties; and they know that the peacemakers are blessed."

(Pike, 313)

While the Princes of Jerusalem are not deciding cases today on the merit of equity and justice, the magistrates and judges of civilized democracies still are taught the canonical law, which teaches the use of just principles. Pike offers the following observation about the realities of work in the present day, versus when it was not merely symbolic in nature. "Forget not these precepts of the old Law; and especially do not forget, as you advance, that every Mason, however humble, is your brother, and the laboring man your peer! Remember always that all Masonry is work, and that the trowel is an emblem of the Degrees in this Council. Labor, when rightly understood, is both noble and ennobling, and intended to develop man's moral and spiritual nature, and not to be deemed a disgrace or a misfortune." Pike, 314) Clearly, we are meant to use the symbolism in this degree and the others for illustrative and teaching purposes; so, that we might develop our own moral and spiritual character.

It's this pursuit that lends itself to what Pike later describes as the "great problem of Humanity." "The great problem of Humanity is wrought out in the humblest abodes; no more than this is done in the highest. A human heart throbs beneath the beggar's gabardine; and that and no more stirs with its beating the Prince's mantle. The beauty of Love, the charm of Friendship, the sacredness of Sorrow, the heroism of Patience, the noble Self-sacrifice, these and their like, alone, make life to be life indeed, and are its grandeur and its power. They are the priceless treasures and glory of humanity; and they are not things of condition. All places and all scenes are alike clothed with the grandeur and charm of virtues such as these." (Pike, 316) Striving to obey the laws of Masonry, by using *equity* and *justice* as a guide, is the purpose of this degree.

A good deal of the Masonic degree's story narratives are necessarily concerned with the *First Temple*, built by King Solomon. The building and reconstruction of the temple, the *Twelve Tribes of Israel*, the exodus and various aspects of the Judaic culture during that time are all closely intertwined. There's departures from the ancient historical record and those which occur in some Masonic allegory, however, it's imperative to understand that the lesson or teaching of a degree is often the reason certain imagery was picked for allegorical reference. There are elements of both which overlap and it's helpful to have a basic understanding of the history of Jerusalem for appreciating the many inclusions into Masonic philosophy. Pike admired qualities from all the religious traditions of the world and is one reason (among many) that so many of them are represented in the themes of the Scottish Rite degrees. He felt they all played an equal part in the realm of divinity and teachings. Any disparity between the biblical or philosophical and historical record in such degrees is often the result of the allegorical theme presented in the degree being chosen, simply because of its effectiveness in presenting the lessons of the degree as a story.

Jerusalem's one of the oldest cities in the world; many historians suggest it's been destroyed twice, been under siege 23 times, been captured and recaptured 44 times, and, attacked 52 times…although numbers vary depending on source. Both the Masonic scholar and those interested in Jewish culture and history will find *Jerusalem* by Simon Sebag Montefiore a most helpful and rewarding book to read.

CHAPTER 12

KNIGHT OF THE EAST AND WEST

The seventeenth-degree of Knight of the East and West is considered the first of the truly philosophical degrees in Scottish Rite. Pike explains this and offers the following narrative concerning this degree in *Morals and Dogma*, "[This is] the beginning of a course of instruction which will fully unveil to you the heart and inner mysteries of Masonry. Do not despair because you have often seemed on the point of attaining the inmost light, and have as often been disappointed. In all time, truth has been hidden under symbols, and often under a succession of allegories: where veil after veil had to be penetrated before the true Light was reached, and the essential truth stood revealed. The Human Light is but an imperfect reflection of a ray of the Infinite and Divine." (Pike, 317) The differentials and symbolism between the religions of the East and those of the West is the purpose of this degree, and, the discussion for this chapter.

"After the intermingling of different nations, which resulted from the wars of Alexander in three-quarters of the globe, the doctrines of Greece, of Egypt, of Persia, and of India, met and intermingled everywhere. All the barriers that had formerly kept the nations apart were thrown down; and while the People of the West readily connected their faith with those of the East, those of the Orient hastened to learn the traditions of Rome and the legends of Athens. While the Philosophers of Greece, all (except the disciples of Epicurus) more or less Platonists, seized eagerly upon the beliefs and doctrines of the East, —the Jews and Egyptians, before then the most exclusive of all peoples, yielded to that eclecticism which prevailed among their masters, the Greeks and Romans." (Pike 318) The intercession of religious traditions sparked debate and clash because of the ignorant but brought together great ideas and symbolism for the educated and enlightened.

Christianity itself has intercessory prayer, which allows for the prayer of others' behalf and a positive example of unity; whilst this practice is meant to encompass persons of one church or faith, it can transcend religious doctrine. In the *First Epistle of Paul* to *Timothy* (which is also known as the *Pastoral Epistles*, a collection of three letters written by the Apostle Paul in the *New Testament*) this practice was encompassed by the following passage and is particularly cited for this regard. "I exhort therefore, that, first-of-all, supplications, prayers, intercessions, and giving of thanks, be made for all men; for kings, and for all that are in authority; that we may lead a quiet and peaceable life in all godliness and honesty." [34]

Pike elaborates on this further, while offering a historical and philosophical dimension. "Accordingly, the distinction between the esoteric and the exoteric doctrine, immemorial in other creeds, easily gained a foothold among many of the Christians; and it was held by a vast number, even during the preaching of Paul, that the writings of the Apostles were incomplete; that they contained only the germs of another doctrine, which must receive from the hands of philosophy, not only the systematic arrangement which was wanting, but all the development which lay concealed therein. The writings of the Apostles, they said, in addressing themselves to mankind in general, enunciated only the articles of the vulgar faith; but transmitted the mysteries of knowledge to superior minds, to the Elect, —mysteries handed down from generation to generation in esoteric traditions; and to this science of the mysteries they gave the name of Γνῶσις Gnōsis in Greek. (Further discussion of the *Mysteries* can be found in Chapter 18)

The Gnostics derived their leading doctrines and ideas from Plato and Philo, the Zend-Avesta and the Kabbalah, and the Sacred books of India and Egypt; and thus, introduced into the bosom of Christianity the cosmological and theosophical speculations, which had formed the larger portion of the ancient religions of the Orient, joined to those of the Egyptian, Greek, and Jewish doctrines, which the Neo-Platonists had equally adopted in the Occident." (Pike, 319)

The difficulty of understanding a previously correct source has long been problematic for Masonry and this, mostly in-itself, led to the distribution and writing of the degree rituals and aides for memory. Despite exercising an exclusively oral tradition upon its inception. Freemasonry began to use writing to transcribe its rituals, whether authorized or not. The same problem of preservation of old concepts and ideas with as little change as possible has existed for most all religions; otherwise there would not be so many versions of the same popular religious texts readily available. Many traditions use allegory and symbolism for explaining similar events or teachings; the integration and appreciation of such lies at the core of understanding this degree's importance. Pike spends a good deal of this degree's chapter in *Morals and Dogma* discussing the influences of different religious sects and their teachings.

In this degree's ritual, the master of the lodge is styled as John the Baptist; a hint to the more popular author by many of *Revelations*, as well as one of the two patron saints of Freemasonry. The *Book of Revelation* spans three literary genres: the apocalyptic, the epistolary and the prophetic. [35] The prophetic vision of the Second Coming of Christ and the contents of this book are well documented elsewhere and their integration therefore isn't important to discussed further in this chapter, however, it's inextricably linked to *Revelations*. There is a "rather complete lack of consensus" among scholars about the structure of *Revelations* [36] however and the debate about its true author (John the Baptist, or another man simply named John as it's originally written) will likely continue indefinitely.

The connection between the *Book of Revelation* and Freemasonry's degrees lies both in enlightenment and in nature itself. "But, whatever may be the teachings in the book of nature to be fairly deduced from it by an enlightened mind, it is to the book of divine revelation that we are mainly indebted for that enlightenment which enables us to study it with intelligence and advantage; it is chiefly from God's Word that we derive our knowledge of His will. Men destitute of the light of revelation, have never liked to retain God in their knowledge, and professing themselves to be wise have become fools, [37] "and changed the glory of the incorruptible God into an image made like unto corruptible men, and to birds, and four-footed beasts and creeping things." [38] Enlightenment is the purpose of education and a proper civil society, which must not exceed its wrongs; if it hopes to maintain the transfer of knowledge required by each generation, for enlightenment to exist in perpetuity.

Paton continues, "To God's Word we must look for a perfect knowledge of our duty and the direction of our conduct; and, therefore, the symbol which we behold in the trestle board must ever remind us of the value of the Holy Scriptures and the advantage which is to be obtained by searching them diligently and continually. And thus, this symbol directs us to the great light of Masonry, and reminds us that we ought always to seek to avail ourselves of that light, and by it to view all things concerning our conduct and duty." (Paton, 111)

The *Book of Revelation* is meant to symbolically present the message that we should have faith that God will prevail in end time scenarios [39] and, as a basis to help shape proper conduct. The dark, apocalyptic message in the letters contained in *Revelations* is a means of encouraging enlightenment amongst nature; painting an ominous picture of what existence is like without much of the populace governing their conduct in a manner acceptable to both Eastern or Western religious traditions' tenets. We must always strive to remember not only just our brethren, but also the others we may so encounter in our travels who have different faiths than our own. This degree is not merely concerned with the toleration of the various religious traditions, but more in understanding that the allegory and symbolism from each can be appreciated equally; in this sense, Masonry can teach religion without being one.

Hutchens explains this corollary exceptionally well in *A Bridge to*

Light. "It is important to stress, however, that the symbolism is borrowed to teach different lessons from those taught in the *Book of Revelation* itself. These lessons are not intended to replace those of any faith but are rather simple opportunities for further instruction on the importance of moral rectitude. For example, the *Book of Seven Seals* used in the ceremony of the degree of Knight of the East and West is but a symbol to encourage the candidates to study what the *Book of Revelation* teaches. Only Christ is worthy to open that Book, and in the ritual, the *Book of Seven Seals* remains closed throughout. Such symbols are to be viewed as analogies and not equivalencies. Masonry does not teach the falseness of any faith—all are equally respected and honored by the Fraternity. Each candidate is expected to reserve unto himself the tenets and teachings of his faith, and, most importantly, to live them. (Hutchens, 129) In this vein, the degree ritual should not be viewed as a substitute for religious interpretation or meanings, but rather as a reminder of the importance of truth to Masonry; that the judgment of individual persons is for the God of their religious tradition.

CHAPTER 13

KNIGHT ROSE CROIX

The eighteenth-degree of Knight Rose Croix is the final of the four degrees contained in the Chapter Rose Croix. The importance and symbolism of the passion cross is examined in this chapter; which we learn is not unique to any religion. This chapter also discusses the false myth that the *Rosicrucian Order* and the Masonic degrees of the Rose Croix are related, and, more information about their relations and origins. Pike wasn't concerned with the fascinating history of the Rose Croix degrees development, nor its alignment with the Rosicrucian's, hence its inclusion here. "When this Degree had its origin, it is not important to inquire; nor with what different rites it has been practiced in different countries and at various times. It is of very high antiquity." (Pike, 361) The complexity of doing so likely outweighed the importance of discussing the symbolism and universal religious application in the degree, which Pike spends a good deal of the degree's chapter in *Morals and Dogma* covering. The importance of both the red rose and the pelican offering its flesh (to its young for nourishment) are covered extensively in this degree's lecture by Pike, and, in a substantial number of other works; thus, its exclusion here.

It's helpful to understand the basic purpose of the Knight Rose Croix degree before delving further into discussion about the passion (or red) cross and the general origins of the degree's philosophy. Pike summarizes this well in *Morals and Dogma*. "The Degree of Rose teaches three things; —the unity, immutability and goodness of God; the immortality of the Soul; the ultimate defeat and extinction of evil and wrong and sorrow, by a Redeemer or Messiah, yet to come, if he has not already appeared. It replaces the three pillars of the old Temple, with three that have already been explained to you, —Faith [in God, mankind, and man's self], Hope [in the victory over evil, the advancement of Humanity, and a hereafter], and Charity [relieving the wants and tolerant of the errors and faults of others]. To be trustful to be hopeful, to be indulgent; these, in an age of selfishness, of ill opinion of human nature, of harsh and bitter judgment, are the most important Masonic Virtues, and the true supports of every Masonic Temple. And they are the old pillars of the Temple under different names. For he only is wise who judges others charitably; he only is strong who is hopeful; and there is no beauty like a firm faith in God, our fellows and ourselves." (Pike, 359)

While the red cross is essentially a mystery of the *Second Temple* added to that of Solomon, "the Rosy Cross of Harodim is the erection of a spiritual temple not made with hands, the Mystery of the ancient Gnostics – "God with us" in the bodily temple." [40] The *Rosicrucian Order* owes its origins to the Gnostics, [41] which are discussed in detail in the chapter devoted to the twenty-third degree. The passion or red cross predates Christianity and has a universal connotation as a symbol of life; both its emanation from deity and the hope of eternal life, which comes from faith in the goodness of deity, regardless of name. The passion cross also serves as a reminder that Masonry favors no religion over another and uses its symbols concerning divinity to be of universal application, regardless of origin. Pike expands on this further in this degree's chapter in *Morals and Dogma*. "The Cross has been a sacred symbol from the earliest antiquity. It is found upon all the enduring monuments of the world, in Egypt, in Assyria, in Hindustan, in Persia, and on the Buddhist towers of Ireland. The Druids cut an oak into its shape and held it sacred, and built their temples in that form. Pointing to the four quarters of the world, it was the symbol of universal nature. It was on a cruciform tree, that Krishna was said to have expired, pierced with arrows. It was revered in Mexico.

But, its peculiar meaning in this degree is that given to it by the Ancient Egyptians. Thoth or Phtha is represented on the oldest monuments carrying in his hand the Crux Ansata, or *Ankh*, [a Tau cross, with a ring or circle over it]. He is so seen on the double tablet of Shufu and Noh Shufu, builders of the greatest of the pyramids, at Wady Meghara, in the peninsula of Sinai. It was the hieroglyphic for life, and with a triangle prefixed meant life giving. To us therefore it is the symbol of Life—of that life that "emanated from the Deity, and of that Eternal Life for which all hope; through our faith in God's infinite goodness." (Pike, 362) The rosy cross was also used extensively by the Rosicrucian's and remains an important element of symbolism to this philosophy today. This is the visual element that many quickly identify with existing in both Rosicrucianism and Masonic work; thus, making the false connotation that both are also directly related somehow. It's known that both groups use the same philosophical and symbolical meanings from the rosy cross, but in truth aren't related; despite some members belonging to both organizations, particularly in the late nineteenth century.

While similarities exist in some shared doctrines, the *Rosicrucian Order* and the Masonic degrees of the Rose Croix are not related and didn't directly influence each other, despite both existing in the United States. Consider the following excerpt from this letter on December 16, 1912 to A.P. Worthington from R.S. Clymer: "In America, there *was no Society, Order, or Fraternity bearing the name Rosicrucian before* Dr. P.B. Randolph *founded the Rosicrucian Fraternity in its triple form.* The Masonic body, when the Scottish Rite began to be worked, had a degree known as the Rose Croix as they have now; but this must not be confused with the *Rosicrucian Order*, since it is purely Masonic and purely a Ritualistic Degree, making no pretense of inner teachings. Up to a few years ago, the *Rosicrucian Order*, or Fraternity, founded by Dr. Randolph, *was the only one existing in America.* Since then, the Rosicrucian…has been started, which, I understand, is teaching Theosophy under that name."

Some twenty years ago, the *English Masonic Rose Cross* began to do work in America, but that was given up entirely after the first attempt. Dr. Randolph used different names: such as, *Rosicrucian's, Rosy Cross, Rose Cross* and the *Hierarch of the Rose Cross.* The title Rose Croix is purely Masonic." [42] The *Royal Order of Scotland* is also a Masonic group and one of its two degrees is called the *Rosy Cross*, which exists today as an honors society and shall be discussed in more detail below. Finally, the beginnings of the Rose Croix degree conferred in today's Scottish Rite lies in the French *Grade of Rose Croix*, which was first known in 1747; "it is probable that the Rose Croix degree has been borrowed from the *Rosy Cross of the Scottish Royal Order of Heredom*, but in passing from Scotland to France it greatly changed its form and organization, as it resembles in no respect its archetype, except that both are eminently Christian in their design." [43] It's important noting that the oldest known authentic Rose Croix degree was in 1760 and called *Le chevalier de l'aigle souverain de Rose Croix de Strasboug.* [44]

"The next point is that the *Rosy Cross* has perhaps some shadowy analogies with the *French Grade of Rose Croix*, but is in no sense the same ritual, with however grave variations. There would be, for this reason, more than temerity in the suggestion that the one was copied from the other, or that the one originated from the other. It is probable to my own mind that they sprang from a common root, which is to be sought in the literary memorials concerning the *Rosicrucian Brotherhood*, and that in respect of the *Royal Order* it seems to draw from that branch of the memorials which dwells more especially on the cross ensanguined by the blood of the Redeemer than from that which is concerned with the Red Rose uplifted in the center of the Cross. The matter of the symbolism is in one case rather the sacrifice of Messiahs, who shed His blood for man, and in the other it is rather the mystical resurrection, which followed the sacrifice. I consider that the *Rose Croix* Grade is by far the more important of the two in the depth of its intimations; but on the questions of date, origin and relations there is no first and second in the interest." [45]

It's both informative and helpful to consider the non-Masonic Rosicrucian's development in understanding their "related, but completely different" relevance to Scottish Rite. The *Rosicrucian Order* did not come to the United States until 1909, when American H. Spencer Lewis traveled to France and was initiated into the *Rosicrucian Order*. Lewis took on the task of renewing interest in Rosicrucianism in the United States, where it had ceased to be practiced after being first established in Philadelphia in 1694. [46] The use of the name and similar philosophies by other groups has also caused a great deal of confusion for the casual observer. While Freemasons may have also been members of Rosicrucian-related groups, for example, they were not related to the *Rosicrucian Order*. The following passage from Lewis explains this important distinction well.

"We do find, however, that preceding the year 1870 the development of Freemasonic activity in England, with an increasing desire on the Continent to add more and higher degrees to the existing Masonic degrees, tempted many men of that organization to establish separate secret bodies or societies composed entirely of Masons, and in some cases new Orders or organizations were established with many degrees based upon Masonic symbols and requiring Masonic affiliations as a prerequisite for affiliation in the new organization. The histories of Freemasonry deal extensively with this unfortunate situation throughout Europe, for these many bodies attaching themselves with the Freemasonic ideals cased endless trouble and confusion. A few of the bodies thus formed became recognized eventually and carried on a very excellent work. It must be stated, however, that the average Freemasonic enthusiast of that period was a true seeker for *light* and arcane wisdom, and while he found much in the Freemasonic teachings to gratify his desires or satiate his hunger, many seemed to feel that there was more *light* and wisdom to be found elsewhere and especially in the secret, *mystic* schools which had their origin in the Oriental philosophies. Probably in those days, as today, many of those in the Freemasonic fraternity did not realize the vast amount of wisdom that is contained in their symbology and in their carefully veiled teachings.

However so, the fact remains that many of the most prominent Freemasons congregated at different times in different places, and formed research bodies or groups devoted to the sole purpose of unearthing such additional teachings or arcane knowledge as might be found in the various mystic schools of the day." (Lewis, 128) Even today, one could argue that a good deal of the philosophical knowledge and symbolism (in both the symbolic lodge and appendant bodies, such as Scottish Rite) is not always well understood by all its members, regardless of their efforts and good intentions. The *Hermetic Order of the Golden Dawn* typified the cross-pollination that began between the various Rosicrucian-based orders and those of Masonic bodies in the nineteenth and early twentieth century, or *Golden Dawn* as is more commonly used. Three Freemasons founded this organization in 1887; they were William Woodman, William Westcott and Samuel Liddell Macgregor Mathers, who were also members of another group called *Societas Rosicruciana* in Anglia (or *S.R.I.A*).

The *Golden Dawn* was based on initiation like Masonic bodies, but women could participate equally with men. This would certainly not be considered a regular or recognized Masonic body in modern times. The *Golden Dawn* are most widely known for inspiring what would later become the Thelema and Wicca religious traditions, as well as much of twentieth century Western occultism. [47] Styling itself much like the symbolic Masonic lodge, they had three orders. The first used the Hermetic kabbalah for personal philosophical development, as well as astrology, geomancy and tarot divination. The second order was styled *Rosae Rubeae et Aureae Crucis* (or, the *Ruby Rose* and *Cross of Gold*) and contemplated alchemy, astral travel and scrying, among other forms of magic. Finally, the third order was known as the *Secret*

Chiefs; they mostly concerned themselves with directing the activities of the lower two orders.

Samuel Liddell Macgregor Mathers
SOURCE: Aleister Crowley's Autobiography

The foundation that preceded the *Golden Dawn* however was the *Societas Rosicruciana* in Anglia, a Christian Masonic order founded by Robert Wentworth Little in 1865. [48] Both the structure and grades of this order were derived from eighteenth century *German Order of the Golden and Rosy Cross*, and, became the basis for which the *Golden Dawn* used in 1888 as well. [49] The first order met in a college, which was equivalent to a Masonic lodge. The second order was equivalent to a Provincial Grand Lodge, with the third and final order being equivalent to a Grand Lodge. Much of the *Societas Rosicruciana* in Anglia structure was carried into the *Golden Dawn* and influenced an occult revival with the removal of the requirement that only Christian men who were Freemasons could join.

Those interested in the Rosicrucian Order and its development will immensely enjoy *Rosicrucian Trilogy: Fama Fraternitatis, 1614: Confessio Fraternitatis, 1615: The Chemical Wedding of Christian Rosenkreuz, 1616* by Joscelyn Godwin, Christopher McIntosh and Donate Pahnke McIntosh. This book details the three oldest known Rosicrucian documents, as alluded in its lengthy title. The *Reformation* influenced the Rosicrucian's, who in-turn influenced Masonry and the Rose Croix degrees of Scottish Rite.

CHAPTER 14

THE SYMBOLISM OF THE GRAND PONTIFF DEGREE

The nineteenth-degree continues the use of symbolism derived from the vision of St. John, which began in the seventeenth-degree. It also prepares the candidate to receive instruction about impartiality, which is persistent later in the twenty-first degree of Noachite or Prussian Knight. This chapter explores the symbolism of this degree, and, the virtues necessary in our individual efforts to sow some seeds of goodness for those who come after us. The name of this degree is derived from the Latin word *ponti* (meaning bridge) and *facere*, meaning, "to make" hence the term "bridge builder" and the meaning of Grand Pontiff; a term often associated with the degree,

The candidate is received as a Knight Rose Croix, who's had the special duty to fight intolerance and oppression, while being armed only with *faith, hope* and *charity*. The twelve columns situated around the council chamber in this degree each contain an initial of the *Twelve Tribes of Israel*, are representative of the zodiac, and, the various names of God, as shown in the comparison on the following page. Note the relevance of each tribe being associated with a zodiac sign.

EPHRAIM	**TAURUS**
BENJAMIN	**GEMINI**
ISSACHAR	**CANCER**
JUDAH	**LEO**
NAPHTALI	**VIRGO**
ASHER	**LIBRA**
DAN	**SCORPIO**
MANASSEH	**SAGITTARIUS**
ZEBULON	**CAPRICORN**
REUBEN	**AQUARIUS**
SIMEON	**PISCES**
GAD	**ARIES**

Since the *Book of Revelation* (*7:4-8* specifically) notes that only 12,000 of each tribe were saved from destruction, the chosen represented the most righteous of humanity. The importance of these tribes is thus reinforced with a column and initial of each engraved upon it. The darkness and silence, which then surround the candidate, is broken only by the verbal imagery of the final apocalyptic battle of "good vs. evil" which is presented in the *Revelation to St. John*. The candidate is then made a priest of the *Order of Melchizedek* and expected to exert the priestly qualities of *equitability, justice, sincerity, tolerance* and *truth*.

This degree teaches that a person's actions act as a bridge to both their own immortality, and, the successes (or failures) of future generations. The newly initiated pontiff then symbolically destroys *error, falsehood* and *intolerance* with *charity, honesty, honor* and *truth*. The twelve names of God, when translated from Hebrew, represent their various powers and qualities. They help explain the mystical Kabbalistic symbolism, which Albert Pike inserted into the degrees' lecture to associate with the apocalypse described in the *Book of Revelation.*

While this degree leans heavily on a biblical text and Kabbalistic mysticism, the title of "Grand Pontiff" is not representative of any religious leader or figure. In previous ritual versions, this degree has also been known as Sublime Scottish Mason, particularly in the nineteenth century. The symbolism in this degree refers (overall) to building the New City, where mankind will live together per the principles of Freemasonry. This represents a departure from the overall theme (in the preceding degrees) of building the Temple. The triumph of good over evil will eventually cause such a utopian society to exist again, however, this degree reminds us that "building bridges" is important in life to maintain it, along with the priestly virtues previously mentioned. A society not only remains healthy by exuding these virtues, it ensures successive generations may remain healthy, thus perpetuating a cycle of virtue. It's hard for one to doubt these efforts when this wisdom can be observed looking backwards in history during its highest points of social success.

CHAPTER 15

MASTER OF THE SYMBOLIC LODGE

The Master of the Symbolic Lodge is charged with the special duty of dispensing light and knowledge, while practicing *justice, truth and toleration.* They are further charged with practicing Masonic virtues both inside and outside of lodge, serving as a good example for others to follow. The hangings of the lodge room are adorned in blue and gold, to serve as a reminder of the clouds in which God appeared before Moses. They remind us that all Masons are equal, even if they belong to only a symbolic lodge and not the Scottish or York Rites, or other Masonic bodies.

The lodge room, symbolism and degree ritual is reminiscent of a "blue" or symbolic lodge, especially with the heavy usage of pillars, squares and triangles. Pike felt the twentieth degree represented a dramatic statement of the "primitive purity" of Masonry. In *Morals and Dogma*, Pike states that, "As a Grand Master of all Symbolic Lodges, it is your special duty to aid in restoring Masonry to its primitive purity. You have become an instructor." (Pike, 399) Pike then summarizes Scottish Rite Masonry very well (in general) while continuing his discourse about the duties of a Master of the symbolic lodge, "We teach the truth of none of the legends we recite. They are to us but parables and allegories, involving and enveloping Masonic instruction; and vehicles of useful and interesting information. They represent the different phases of the human mind, its efforts and struggles to comprehend nature, God, the government of the Universe, the permitted existence of sorrow and evil. Everyone being at liberty to apply our symbols and emblems as he thinks most consistent with truth and reason and with his own faith, we give them such an interpretation only as may be accepted by all." (Pike, 403)

In the first section of the degree ritual, the nine candles in the lodge room are lit one at a time by the candidate to represent the *nine great lights in Masonry; veneration, charity, generosity, heroism, honor, patriotism, justice, toleration* and *truth*. The Tracing Board in this degree has five great squares, with three giant triangles surrounding an octagon. The candidate learns these are representative of the *twenty-nine virtues*. Printed on the squares are *prudence, temperance, chastity* and *sobriety, heroism, firmness, equanimity* and *zeal, probity, honor, fidelity* and *punctuality, disinterestedness, lenity, forgiveness* and *forbearance, charity, kindness, generosity* and *liberality*. The triangles represent gratitude to God, love of mankind and confidence in human nature, veneration of God, devotedness to family and friends and patriotism. The virtues considered the most important are reserved for the triangle in the top center of the octagon, which are *justice, truth* and *toleration*.

The most profound feedback concerning a Masters duty from Pike comes from the Venerable Masters lecture during the first section. "My Brother, as the presiding officer of a Lodge, it will be your particular duty to dispense light and knowledge to the Brethren. Those duties are not performed by merely giving or cause to be given a lecture for the instruction of the Brethren. Nor is it accomplished by asking and receiving the answers to merely formal and trivial questions. On the contrary, that duty is far higher and more important; and it behooves the Master to be prepared to perform it. No one should accept the office of Master, until, by acquaintance and familiarity with the history, morals and philosophy of Masonry he is fitted to enlighten and instruct the Brethren…" (De Hoyos, 514)

It's important to also understand that the importance of this degree goes far beyond the symbolic imagery inherent in the *nine great lights of Masonry*, or the *twenty-nine virtues*. These elements of the symbolic lodge that most Masons attend are important in themselves; however, their presence is also used to explain and highlight both the importance and responsibility placed in the hands of the Master of a lodge…whether it's a symbolic lodge, an appendant body like Scottish Rite, or, a leadership position of importance outside Masonry which includes directing others. The easiest way to envision this is a director or executive of a large company, or similarly, the owner of a family farming business that employs others in the region to tend their fields and bring their produce to market. The extension of Masonic virtues into the application of one's life is the goal of any philosophy or progressive science; in this degree's instance, Pike's explaining (albeit in different language) that our responsibilities to others as a leader should always be in the forefront of our mind; especially when contemplating decisions affecting the wellbeing of others placed in our charge. The level of engagement matters not (in theory) between the owner of a restaurant and the director of a publically traded corporation; while the position description or responsibilities of the job may vary drastically, the idea of exercising Masonic virtues in our management of others remains unchanged.

CHAPTER 16

AN IMPARTIAL JUDICIARY: THE NOACHITE OR PRUSSIAN KNIGHT

The very core of the twenty-first degree is explained in Albert Pikes *Morals and Dogma* as the need for a free and unbiased press; Pike certainly had personal experience as both an attorney and newspaper editor. This isn't possible in a democracy without an impartial judiciary, which ensures freedoms are not abridged, censored or otherwise influenced. This chapter explores the requirements for justice to be administered impartially, and, continues upon the concept of "justice as fairness" first espoused by John Rawls in *A Theory of Justice.* The Provost & Judge is taught to act with justice, deliberate with impartiality and decide with equity. A Noachite or Prussian Knight is further instructed to be devoted to the cause of everyone who has been wronged by the great or oppressed by the powerful, those unjustly accused, those who've suffered from bribery or corrupt judges, orphans, widows and finally, those distressed or destitute.

Being successful as an impartial judge liberates one from the illusion that accumulating wealth is necessarily the purpose of human existence. We're taught to temper justice with mercy in this degree, because there's no man alive who doesn't err and sin. Accordingly, in rendering all judgments a special care must be taken to judge of others actions and motives by the same rules in which they judge themselves. In understanding the illusion of wealth, the Prussian Knight frees themselves from the temptations of bribery, and, from being corrupted by the wealthy. This ensures that no one individual (ideally) is beyond the scales of justice and immune to the punishments for the crimes they may have committed.

The most valuable tool in the hands of a Prussian Knight is that of a "veil of ignorance." The concept of the veil of ignorance was first espoused by John Rawls, who's widely considered the father of social contract theory, and, an important contributor to the concept of distributive justice. Rawls was trying to understand the varied problems of justice when he realized that all humans are born without knowing their future utility in life. This means, for instance, one could become a doctor later in their life and save countless lives, or, could become a criminal who deprives others instead. There's no ability to judge ones later merits or utility at birth, or even at a young age, hence the Prussian Knight wears a veil to remain cognizant of this important distinction when rendering judgments. Rawls used formulas and lexical ordering to make an empirical argument for this concept, which remains valid today. Rawls wasn't concerned merely with the problem of being impartial in a tribunal (as in this degree's ritual) but rather the overall problem of *justice as fairness.* The newly obligated Prussian Knight will undoubtedly find *A Theory of Justice* by Rawls a most helpful text in understanding the degree, as well as a more complete understanding of the Provost & Judge degree.

Rawls offers an empirical basis for understanding the concept of justice as fairness, while Pikes chapter in *Morals and Dogma* offers a normative argument. Pike's concerned with the much narrower focus of being an impartial judge, where Rawls uses an entire book to contemplate the much broader overall concept of distributive justice. As such, it's important to understand why Pike advocates a free and unbiased press in a degree focused on a secret tribunal developed during the Middle Ages, when many were illiterate. We teach the concept of "checks and balances" in American primary schools when explaining the purpose for having a dedicated branch of the government for the judiciary. In countries without a free and unbiased press, the judiciary is seldom transparent; the state doesn't want its abuses and improprieties to be known to the citizenry. Those who don't agree with the oligarchy, or ruling elite are publicized unfavorably in the press, while those of special privilege enjoy immunity from the laws the populace is expected to follow.

Given this, it's easy to understand why the secret *Vehmgericht tribunal* (which met in secret and wielded extraordinary power) in earlier Germanic times was chosen for usage in this degree. Pike explains on pages 18-9 of *Legenda and Readings of the Ancient and Accepted Scottish Rite of Freemasonry* why their power and authority still ultimately failed at the end of the fifteenth century, "Such power placed in human hands without the protecting check of publicity and responsibility could not long exist without misuse. In the great development and extension of the association, it could not be avoided but that unworthy individuals should be received as members who used the power confided to them for the sole satisfaction of their revengeful and baser passions." Pike's also trying to explain that even if a secret court or tribunal is established with the very best intentions, the institution will allow its future members to make biased unlawful judgments, without fear of reproach. The purpose and varied symbolism of the secret tribunal in this degree serves as a reminder that we may not know the character of those judging us and similarly, we must act unbiased and keep the ideals of justice before our own interests.

For further reflection, consider the application of this degree's lesson with the *Foreign Intelligence Surveillance Court*, which was created by the United States Congress in 1978. Its stated purpose is for the, "approval of electronic surveillance, physical search, and certain other forms of investigative actions for foreign intelligence purposes." [50] While the governments required by law to report in writing to the court any activity granted by it which may have violated the law, its decisions, proceedings (and the reasoning used to solicit the courts authority by others) and other modes of operation are largely secret and not available for public disclosure. Is having a modern secret court with legal oversight enough to ensure it doesn't operate like the *Vehmgericht tribunal* did? How would Pike feel about the *Foreign Intelligence Surveillance Court* of the present day, given the lessons of this degree? Would Pike feel that the authority of such a court would suffer abuse from the lack of a "protecting check of publicity" or not having enough public transparency?

It's quite likely that despite the good intentions of oversight instated by Congress in 1978, Pike would still observe such a court as being subject to unlawful bias and judgments. The mention of those unjustly accused, those suffering from bribery or corrupt judges, orphans, widows and finally, those distressed or destitute, highlight the need to also consider impartiality outside of the court room in our daily judgments of others.

CHAPTER 17

THE VIRTUES OF WORK: KNIGHT ROYAL AXE, PRINCE OF LIBANUS

The very foundation of Freemasonry seeks to teach *equality, morality* and *truth* to all men who join the fraternity; that they may be a good and shining example for others who're not Masons to follow. Thus, the incumbent Mason must strive to be patient and determined, not ignorant and always be quick to explain the dignity and importance of labor to those who may seek the wisdom of its lesson. These principles comprise the teachings of both the twenty-second degree of Scottish Rite Freemasonry, and, the degree ritual itself. This chapter will examine the virtue of work and its impact on this degree.

We know from the teachings of this degree that all work is noble and sacred; which is why the purpose (it brings) is sought for most of our lives as adults, and then once again, in our struggle for meaning (or purpose) after retirement. How often do we encounter somebody we've known for many years struggle with identity (or lingering doubts about their purpose) issues after they retire? How often do we then see retired people's volunteer or spend measured amounts of their time on a regular basis doing tasks which they have expertise or interest? The latter scenario is one those who've received the wisdom of the twenty-second degree (whether they're a Mason, or not) tend to embrace, instead of sitting on their front porch in a rocking chair for their remaining existence.

The quintessential example many may recall is Tom Hanks' character in the film Forrest Gump; he'd been so successful in his working career he simply no longer needed to work; yet he mowed several huge lawns with a riding tractor without compensation. Forrest Gump was not the most intellectually gifted individual, yet he learned that what most of us seek must be earned, and, that even when we feel compelled to no longer toil in regular labors, that we should continue to help civilization progress by using our knowledge and talents to foster the virtues of work to younger generations; so, that the cycle may continue as time passes. It matters not what utility the fruits of this labor yield, as it can be teaching children to read, volunteering in a library, or, mowing the grass. Forrest Gump earned the ability to mow lawns with a riding tractor through the utility of his working career; otherwise, he couldn't have afforded to do so. If Forrest hadn't been a war hero and involved in creating a huge company and other notable investments (such as Apple Computer) he probably couldn't have afforded to simply mow grass for free as a young retiree. It's undeniable that Forrest Gump learned both the principles of work and the lessons of the twenty-second degree very well, without being a Freemason.

Man, has labored for much of its existence and the overall challenge (or problem) has remained the same today as it was in prehistoric times; attempt to move civilizations progress ahead enough that it remains relevant (and useful) after our existence is over. Sometimes, this labor is individual in nature and sometimes it's a team effort, but the Egyptian pyramids and the discovery of penicillin are both "shining star" examples, as their usefulness (or utility) has outlived the labor that originally generated them. If society did not have a means to develop its ideas and labor into work, it'd simple cease to exist.

The symbolism in this degree is closely tied with the virtues of work itself; the large axe alone is a reminder of this, and, is prominent in the ritual for this reason. The plane symbolizes (both in Masonry and in the degree ritual) the removal of ignorance with its use; as it smoothens the rough edges and makes an imperfect item far more perfect than before it was used. Such is the principal of this degree, and, the continuity of a healthy utopian society, which can demonstrate signs of improvement after each successive generation. As Rex Hutchens notes in the *Bridge to Light* chapter on this degree, "The axe is nobler than the sword. Masonry hews at those mighty trees, *intolerance, bigotry, superstition, uncharitableness* and *idleness*, thereby letting in the light of truth and reason upon the human mind, which these vices have darkened for centuries." A further study of the initials engraved on the axe reveals persons involved in the use of the cedars of Lebanon for the "holy enterprises" of man's divinity, which include important efforts of labor, such as the rebuilding of the Temple in Jerusalem, Noah's Ark and the Ark of the Covenant itself. Forrest Gump serves as a fine example of an individual wielding the axe of labor correctly, and, integrating the purpose of work itself properly. One needn't be brilliant, or, have extraordinary talents to make a difference with their labor.

A point to consider in interpreting this degree is that all work's noble and sacred; the utility one provides through honest labor shouldn't necessarily be compared against the job being performed. The principles of this degree also teach that the benefit gained by such work by the individual is always equal. Forrest Gump benefits from cutting large fields of grass just the same as a professional athlete does.

CHAPTER 18

CHIEF OF THE TABERNACLE

This chapter explores the importance and purpose of the twenty-sixth degree, which is entitled Chief of the Tabernacle and educates the initiate about the *Lesser Mysteries* throughout ancient Egyptian, Greek and Indian history. This is not only a preparatory degree (to prepare the initiate for the *Greater Mysteries* in the next degree, Prince of the Tabernacle, and the reason these two degrees have never been combined) but it's also a degree of great importance that's rarely staged in most Orients. This is unfortunate, because this degree alludes to the development of what eventually become the three degrees of the "blue" or symbolic lodge of Freemasonry. Pike spends a good deal of this degree's chapter in *Morals and Dogma* discussing the historical background of the *Lesser Mysteries* and initiations, stating the degree's purpose as, "the moral lesson of which is, devotion to the service of God, and disinterested zeal and constant endeavor for the welfare of men." (Pike, 441) Pike also explains the origin and purpose behind the construction of the ancient pyramids in Egypt, which relate directly to the three symbolic degrees conferred today.

The Egyptians are the oldest source of the *Mysteries*. The Moon God Thoth originally presided over Egyptian events and rituals, until he eventually became the god of wisdom, magic and the measurement and regulation of events and time.[51] Thoth also became the father of hieroglyphics, math, medicine and music. He decided it prudent to disseminate his knowledge to others who might be worthy of someday assuming the throne, thus creating what Pike called the *Priests of the*

Living God. This group of initiates learned the arts and sciences from Thoth and promised to not reveal them to others who weren't worthy enough to receive them, thus creating the first formal rites of initiation. Thoth was depicted in several forms, some which differ greatly.

Having initiation ceremonies required a secure area, which could often be used at night; occurring in temples or even underground at times. This, Pike notes, was the original function of the pyramids in ancient Egypt, "The pyramids were probably used for the purposes of initiation, as were caverns, pagodas, and labyrinths; for the ceremonies required many apartments and cells, long passages and wells. In Egypt, a principal place for the *Mysteries* was the island of Philæ on the Nile, where a magnificent Temple of Osiris stood, and where his relics were said to be preserved." Academics and historians have long debated the original purpose of the pyramids in ancient Egypt, with many of them neglecting the study of ancient Egyptians initiation rites into the *Lesser Mysteries.*

Secrecy was always required for all participants of the *Eleusinian Mysteries,* which correlate to the *Mysteries* Pike contemplates in *Morals and Dogma.* It mattered not whether a participant was a new initiate, or a seasoned practitioner; secrecy was used to enforce a division in the populace—between those worthy of such higher knowledge and the masses of others who were deemed unworthy. The traditions were transmitted throughout time by direct teachings in secured areas; where one could not in any way come upon viewing instruction not meant for them. The passages inside the pyramids appear to allow for seeing persons before they can approach too closely, which agrees with this tradition.

Exactly four categories of the populace could partake in the *Mysteries* and enter such reserved areas:

1. Hierophants, priests and priestesses.
2. New initiates who've been deemed worthy.
3. Any who'd attained ἐποπτεία (or contemplation) and had mastered the *Mysteries*.
4. Any who'd participated once and were returning for more study.

The stringent care taken in keeping such higher education from the broad populace was undoubtedly a means of control; thus, nothing was written down for later examination. Hippolytus of Rome, writing in the early 3rd century CE, stated about this point in *Refutation of All Heresies* (or Κατὰ πασῶν αἱρέσεων ἔλεγχος in Greek) that, "the Athenians, while initiating people into the Eleusinian rites, likewise display to those who are being admitted to the highest grade at these mysteries, the mighty, and marvelous, and most perfect secret suitable for one initiated into the highest mystic truths: *an ear of grain in silence reaped.*" [52] The secrecy directive which was so persistent in the administration of (what we'd deem higher education in the modern era) the *Mysteries* undoubtedly required a large confined space that the Egyptian pyramids was perfectly suited. The oral tradition which caused this knowledge to persist into the Egyptian era no doubt brought some challenge in a large expansive desert. The pyramids offered security and protection from the weather, and, were largely constructed by the masses who were not initiated in the teachings occurring inside, however, history shows that slaves and women were sometimes initiated; if they hadn't committed murder and could speak Greek. [53] This began during the rule of Peisistratos, who was the son of Hippocrates. Thus, the pyramids size allowed for a veritable Egyptian university, especially given the constraints of eligibility. This historical narrative no doubt assisted Pike in reaching his conclusion about the pyramids and is present in the deeper meaning of this degree. Examining Pike's writings offers no context as to whether his interpretation of the pyramids use was solely for the *Mysteries*, or, complemented other uses. Pike's guidance on the pyramids is often missed by those who've read *Morals and Dogma*, hence its inclusion in this chapter.

Most who even recognize Thoth's image typically acknowledge him only for being married to Ma 'at, and, for standing prominently with her on Ra's boat. [54] Many aren't aware that Thoth is also the father of initiation rites, which were included into the degrees of Freemasonry over a very long period. Many espouse the popular notion that the three symbolic degrees (Entered Apprentice, Fellowcraft and Master Mason) were derived from the Knights Templar, when in fact, they're far older and originate with the *Egyptian Mysteries*. "There was a close connection between the story of the captivity of Egypt, the use of the cubit as a unit of measurement, and the Solomonic temple. The main influences in the Egyptization of Continental Lodges seem to have been Count Alessandro Cagliostro (1743-95) and Karl Friedrich Köppen (author of *Crata Repoa* [1778]). Cagliostro became Grand Master of a Parisian Lodge to which a temple of Isis was attached, and his rituals were speedily in some French and Central European Lodges.

In any case, it is clear from standard designs for Masonic Certificates on the Continent that the Egyptian elements were well to the fore. Pyramids, Egyptian columns, palm-trees, sphinxes, and Egyptian Isis or Hathor- headed capitals are much in evidence. From the description of the "Egyptian" rites it seems they were supposed to have been derived from Isiac ceremonies in Ancient Egypt and the Greco-Roman world." [55]

Pike elaborates further on the history and practice of the *Egyptian Mysteries*, "All persons were initiated into the *Lesser Mysteries*; but few attained the greater, in which the true spirit of them, and most of their secret doctrines were hidden. The veil of secrecy was impenetrable, sealed by oaths and penalties the most tremendous and appalling. It was by initiation only, that a knowledge of the Hieroglyphics could be obtained, with which the walls, columns, and ceilings of the Temples were decorated, and which, believed to have been communicated to the Priests by revelation from the celestial deities, the youth of all ranks were laudably ambitious of deciphering." The secrecy surrounding the *Mysteries* is only continued in the Masonic degrees for the passwords and means of recognition and not the entire contents and/or teachings themselves, as the ancients did. Where the Egyptians (and later the Greeks) used secrecy for exclusion to their *Mysteries*, it protected the knowledge of the arts and sciences; ensuring only those deemed worthy of the ruling class received them. This is a major departure from the Masonic philosophy within its various degrees and orders, where the knowledge and teachings are intended for anyone with curiosity and interest.

The Egyptians believed in reincarnation and integrated it into their *Mysteries*. Herodotus once said that, "The Egyptians are the first who propounded the theory that the human soul is imperishable, and that when the body of anyone dies it enters into some other body that may be ready to receive it; and that when it has gone the round of all created forms on land, in water, and in the air, then it once more enters the human body born for it; and also that this cycle of existence for the soul takes place in three thousand years." [56] The concept of reincarnation is first presented in the symbolic lodge with the third degree of Master Mason, and, the lessons surrounding it are continued in various Scottish Rite degrees.

The *Mysteries* left Egypt and were first used by the Phoenicians in the city of Tyre, which is in present day Lebanon and was built originally around 2750 BCE as a walled city around the mainland, per Herodotus. [57] Pike explains next how the god Osiris changed his name, which then allowed the *Mysteries* to migrate outside Egypt and Phoenicia, "Osiris changed his name, and become Adoni or Dionysus, still the representative of the Sun; and afterward these *Mysteries* were introduced successively into Assyria, Babylon, Persia, Greece, Sicily, and Italy. In Greece and Sicily, Osiris took the name of Bacchus, and Isis that of Ceres, Cybele, Rhea and Venus." Pike further describes how a varied collection of *Mysteries* was standardized and thus began to further spread, "The *Mysteries of Eleusis*, celebrated at Athens in honor of Ceres, swallowed up, as it were, all the others. All the neighboring nations neglected their own, to celebrate those of Eleusis; and in a little while all Greece and Asia Minor were filled with the Initiates. They spread into the Roman Empire, and even beyond its limits, "those holy and august *Eleusinian Mysteries*," said Cicero, "in which the people of the remotest lands are initiated." Zosimus says that they embraced the whole human race; and Aristides termed them the common temple of the whole world." And thus, the *Mysteries* were in use throughout most of civilization at that time, after starting as an Egyptian initiation rite.

Pike elaborates further on the purpose of the *Mysteries*, from the philosophers Plato and Socrates' perspective, "Plato said that the object of the *Mysteries* was to re-establish the soul in its primitive purity, and in that state of perfection which it had lost. Epictetus said, "whatever is met with therein has been instituted by our Masters, for the instruction of man and the correction of morals." The first philosophy often reverted to the natural mode of teaching; and Socrates is said to have eschewed dogmas, endeavoring, like the *Mysteries*, rather to awaken and develop in the minds of his hearers the ideas with which they were already endowed or pregnant, than to fill them with ready-made adventitious opinions. So, Freemasonry still follows the ancient manner of teaching. Her symbols are the instruction she gives; and the lectures are but often partial and insufficient one-sided endeavors to interpret those symbols. He who would become an accomplished Mason, must not be content merely to hear or even to understand the lectures, but must, aided by them, and they having as it were marked out the way for him, study, interpret, and develop the symbols for himself." Pike's essentially warning the reader about the complexity of symbolism in Scottish Rite degrees, and, to not try to interpret everything in a few sittings. Undoubtedly, the continuation of the *Mysteries* by the Greek and Roman societies solidified them into structured lessons in the fundamentals of the arts and sciences, which continue in the present day in both Freemasonry's degree systems, and, the liberal arts and sciences in undergraduate college study.

Other elements (such as building cities, prayer and the Zodiac) were recorded by the Greeks because of the *Mysteries* per Pike and are of importance. "Bar Hebraeus says Enoch was the first who invented books and different sorts of writing. The ancient Greeks declare that Enoch is the same as Mercury Trismegistus [Hermes], and that he taught the sons of men the art of building cities, and enacted some admirable laws.... He discovered the knowledge of the Zodiac, and the course of the Planets; Gods! The World's Mansion!" (Pike, 134) The concept of "discovering" an art or science was proof of the successful continuation of the *Mysteries* from the Egyptians, regardless of whether the recipients were of a noble rank. This continued the problem the Egyptians already experienced of needing secrecy to conduct and differentiate initiates of the various degrees of the *Lesser and Greater Mysteries*.

The first degree of Freemasonry shares several parallels with the *Mysteries* of the early inhabitants of India. They practiced the Patriarchal religion; before the worship of Vishnu began with Hindu and it's at this point the *Mysteries* begin there as well. The *Mysteries* in India, Pike tells us, were celebrated in underground caverns and grottos where it was naturally dark; which was consistent with the Egyptian pyramids. Pike describes several familiar elements of the Entered Apprentice degrees' initiation, as they were originally derived from the Indian *Mysteries*, "The Initiate was invested with a cord of three threads, so twined as to make three times three, and called *zennar*. Hence comes our cable-tow. It was an emblem of their triune Deity, the remembrance of whom we also preserve in the three chief officers of our Lodges, presiding in the three quarters of that Universe which our Lodges represent; in our three greater and three lesser lights, our three movable and three immovable jewels, and the three pillars that support our Lodges." The *Mysteries* clearly were the original source of much of the content and imagery of the symbolic lodge degrees' ritual. The concept of being in the dark (both physically and philosophically) during the degrees and initiations was the result of using indoor apartments, or, dark underground areas, where illumination was difficult.

After reaching 20 years of age and receiving the probation for the second degree, the Indian *Mysteries* directed that the candidate be taken to a bright cavern, where the three principal Hierophants sat in the east, west and south, representing the Indian Triple Deity. Pike explains what occurred next, "The candidate, thus taught the first great primitive truth was called upon to make a formal declaration, that he would be tractable and obedient to his superiors; that he would keep his body pure; govern his tongue, and observe a passive obedience in receiving the doctrines and traditions of the *Order*, and the firmest secrecy in maintaining inviolable its hidden and abstruse mysteries. Then he was sprinkled with water (whence our baptism); certain words, now unknown, were whispered in his ear; and he was divested of his shoes, and made to go three times around the cavern. Hence our three circuits; hence we were neither barefoot nor shod: and the words were the Pass-words of that Indian Degree." These activities mirror many of those in the third degree of Master Mason in the symbolic lodge. The act of receiving baptism occurs during various Scottish Rite degrees; the Chief of the Tabernacle degree reveals the history of baptisms original usage, during the *Mysteries.*

The Grecian *Mysteries* utilized a three-degree system, as opposed to the four used in the Indian *Mysteries.* Pythagoras taught *arithmetic, astronomy, geometry, grammar, logic, music* and *rhetoric;* all of which are necessary elements of the lecture in the second degree of Fellowcraft in the symbolic lodge. Pike summarizes succinctly the elements of Pythagoras' teachings of the *Mysteries,* which correspond with the second Masonic degree. "Pythagoras taught that the two most excellent things were, to speak the truth, and to render benefits to one another. Particularly he inculcated *Silence, Temperance, Fortitude, Prudence,* and *Justice.* He taught the immortality of the soul, the Omnipotence of God, and the necessity of personal holiness to qualify a man for admission into the Society of the Gods. Thus, we owe the particular mode of instruction in the Degree of Fellowcraft to Pythagoras; and that Degree is but an imperfect reproduction of his lectures." Much of the Fellowcraft degree is a direct result of Pythagoras.

We know that Masonic honors were (fittingly) paid to Pythagoras as the reputed discoverer of the *forty-seventh problem of Euclid* and were often acknowledged in monitors and writings, "This wise philosopher enriched his mind abundantly in a general knowledge of things, and more especially in Geometry and Masonry; on this subject he drew out many problems and theorems, and among the most distinguished he erected this, which, in the joy of his heart, he called *Eureka*, in the Grecian language signifying *"I have found it!"* and upon the discovery of which he is said to have sacrificed a hecatomb." [58] The *forty-seventh problem of Euclid* is acknowledged most especially in the symbolic lodge the candidate being escorted around the lodge room three times during the first degree of Entered Apprentice, four times for the second degree of Fellowcraft and five times for the final degree of Master Mason. While Euclid's problem is discussed briefly during the lecture, it's true history and significance is not revealed (or fully understood) until the Chief of the Tabernacle degree has been conferred and/or studied extensively.

The symbolism in this degree reveals the Masonic significance of the number seven, and, is often missed in favor of discussing the *Twelve Tribes of Israel* and their colorful jeweled insignia on the degree's apron instead. The Venerable High Priest states during the lecture that, "The lamp with seven branches, upon the apron, wrought in gold, represents the seven planets of the ancient world; the sun and the middle, with Mars, Jupiter, and Saturn on one side, and Venus, Mercury, and the moon on the other. It also represents the seven archangels': *Zerachiel, Auriel, Gabriel, Michael, Khamaliel, Raphael* and *Tsaphiel*. Michael was representative with the head of the lion, Auriel with that of an ox, Rafael with the human head and Gabriel with that of an eagle. All the seven are attributes of God. The number seven is a sacred number in many religions. It appears often in the Hebrew writings and in the Apocalypse; and here, particularly in the seven lamps. Under the symbols of the seven planets, which it represents, the ancients figured the seven virtues. Faith—that aspiration towards the infinite, was represented by the sun: hope by the moon, charity by Venus: fortitude—always victorious over rage or anger by Mars: prudence by Mercury, temperance by Saturn and justice by Jupiter." (De Hoyos, 562) The chart below illustrates the symbolic connection that exists between the archangels, planets and Masonic values; united together by the number seven.

FAITH	**SUN**	*TSUPHIEL*
HOPE	**MOON**	*RAPHAEL*
CHARITY	**VENUS**	*MICHAEL*
FORTITUDE	**MARS**	*ZERACHIEL*
PRUDENCE	**MERCURY**	*KHAMAIEL*
TEMPERANCE	**SATURN**	*GABRIEL*
JUSTICE	**JUPITER**	*AURIEL*

There's eight fundamental degrees in Freemasonry; they're the first three degrees of the "blue" or symbolic lodge, and, the Secret Master, Perfect Elu, Prince of Jerusalem, Knight Rose Croix and Knight Kadosh degrees of the Scottish Rite. Given the importance of the history of degrees and initiations themselves contained therein, it's incumbent the Chief of the Tabernacle degree also be considered fundamental; thus, encouraging its performance at degree reunions. Even in large Valleys (or Orients) this degree is too often only communicated at degree reunions; this disadvantages everyone, as the long historical length alone puts the reader at risk of perhaps not discovering the true history and significance of the Masonic degrees themselves. Pike spends 48 pages on this degree alone in *Morals and Dogma* thus, and, his long-winded style of writing is undoubtedly tempting for contemporary readers to skip parts of. Freemasonry inadvertently preserved the very necessities required for the continuation of a just and orderly society, from the formation and preservation of its various degree systems. Thus, it's important to consider presenting a concise, yet detailed description when communicating the degree and not staging it. One could easily argue the Chief of the Tabernacle degree explains why any degrees or initiation rites in the world exist; making it alone worthy of becoming the ninth fundamental degree of Freemasonry.

CHAPTER 19

PRINCE OF THE TABERNACLE

This chapter explores the importance of the twenty-fifth degree, and, continues the theme of the *Lesser Mysteries* introduced in the previous degree with an exploration of the *Greater Mysteries*. The use of symbols as a means of instruction was an important element of the *Greater Mysteries* and paramount in the development of hieroglyphics, and, the integration between written language and sounds. Pike succinctly outlines this history in *Morals and Dogma*, amongst the several pages dedicated to this degree, "All the ideas of the Priests of Hindustan, Persia, Syria, Arabia, Chaldæa, Phœnicia, were known to the Egyptian Priests. The rational Indian philosophy, after penetrating Persia and Chaldæa, gave birth to the Egyptian *Mysteries*. We find that the use of Hieroglyphics was preceded in Egypt by that of the easily understood symbols and figures, from the mineral, animal, and vegetable kingdoms, used by the Indians, Persians, and Chaldeans to express their thoughts; and this primitive philosophy was the basis of the modern philosophy of Pythagoras and Plato." (Pike, 445) The previous degree prepared the candidate to symbolically receive the *Lesser Mysteries*, while the Prince of the Tabernacle degree exposes them to the symbolic instruction of the *Greater Mysteries*. Both degrees are closely related and symbolize a period of several years in-between them, in which the candidate has been engaged in contemplation and further study of the *Mysteries*.

The theme of reincarnation is addressed again in this degree; coupled with the important reminder that initiates of the *Greater Mysteries* were considered the most noble of their peers, thus being worthy to receive the wisdom of the *Mysteries*. Pike elaborates further, "Socrates said, in the Phædo of Plato: "It well appears that those who established the *Mysteries*, or secret assemblies of the initiated, were no contemptible personages, but men of great genius, who in the early ages strove to teach us, under enigmas, that he who shall go to the invisible regions without being purified, will be precipitated into the abyss; while he who arrives there, purged of the stains of this world, and accomplished in virtue, will be admitted to the dwelling-place of the Deity. The initiated are certain to attain the company of the Gods."" Pike also addressed the persistent theme of reincarnation associated with the historical development of the *Mysteries*, "Everywhere, and in all their forms, the *Mysteries* were funereal; and celebrated the mystical death and restoration to life of some divine or heroic personage: and the details of the legend and the mode of the death varied in the different countries where the *Mysteries* were practiced. Their explanation belongs both to astronomy and mythology; and the *Legend of the Master's Degree* is but another form of that of the *Mysteries*, reaching back, in one shape or other, to the remotest antiquity. Whether Egypt originated the legend, or borrowed it from India or Chaldæa, it is now impossible to know. But the Hebrews received the *Mysteries* from the Egyptians; and of course, were familiar with their *legend*, —known as it was to those Egyptian Initiates, Joseph and Moses."

The third-degree Master Mason ritual from the symbolic lodge is the "Master's Degree" which Pike's referring, and, its theme involves the candidate being raised from the dead. This presents an apparent paradox for the newly raised and observant Master Mason, as Freemasonry doesn't prefer one religious tradition to another, yet it uses the concept of reincarnation; an important element of spirituality that's different among most religion. While some blue lodge rooms use the imagery of stars painted on the ceiling, for example, there's no familiar Egyptian decoration (or materials) used throughout its three degrees, like hieroglyphics, etc. The theme of the Master Mason degree isn't Egyptian or Indian either; these are clues not learned or understood until the twenty-fourth and twenty-fifth degrees...much later in Scottish Rite. The brethren of the symbolic lodge don't always understand the truth; that reincarnation was practiced in antiquity with the *Mysteries*, thus being the foundation for the Master Mason ritual and all the degrees in Freemasonry. In the same way, the Perfect Elu degree is most helpful in explaining the answers to important questions not explained (or revealed) in the symbolic lodge, both the Chief and Prince of the Tabernacle degrees are equally helpful in understanding the origin of Freemasonry, it's degrees and rituals. From an overall perspective, the symbolic lodge can also be viewed as a greatly abbreviated, contemporary form of the *Lesser Mysteries*; with the Scottish Rite degrees representing the *Greater Mysteries*. When a Master Mason says, they're joining Scottish Rite to "receive more light," that's essentially what it means; they've received and contemplated the *Lesser Mysteries* in the symbolic lodge and are ready to receive the teachings of the *Greater Mysteries* in Scottish Rite, whether they realize it or not. One can be given all the knowledge that exists; if they cannot understand it, they cannot use it for anything with purpose. This presents a viable, but weak overall argument in support of the Egyptians keeping the *Greater Mysteries* hidden from the common person with interest in them; giving them all the answers without a strong foundation first is a disservice if they can't apply or understand their newfound wisdom. This explains both the necessity and synchronicity of the *Lesser* and *Greater Mystery* degree systems of antiquity.

Reincarnation shares a symbolic connection with the jewel used in this degree, which is simply the Phoenician letter "A" or *aleph*, which is worn around the neck with a narrow, purple cord or ribbon. This letter is also another representation of the pentagram or five-pointed star, as it can also be viewed at any angle and is an initial of Deity in the name of *Adonai*, which means Lord. The five-pointed star has a single point upwards, which represents divinity and symbolizes man's five senses, the five members (the head, arms and legs) and the five fingers on each hand, which are used to signify the tokens used to distinguish Masons. (Hutchens, 199) Further, the first and last letters of the Greek alphabet (Alpha and Omega) are inscribed onto the five-pointed star; this represents the beginning and end of all things. While the Jewish *Torah* appears to be largely a historical narrative, the entire text can be regarded as a mystical name of God. We learn in this regard from the Jewish *Tales of Reincarnation*, that, "Each letter has a unique place in this order, so that the Aleph in one word is not at all the same "energy" as the Aleph in another word. It is this understanding of the *Torah* as a cosmic blueprint that enables us to comprehend a story like "The Soul of Ruth," where the proof of Ruth's reincarnation in a European rabbi is based upon specific letters in the biblical text." [59] The use of a specific letter for symbolism of all collective languages and traditions is a practice of Freemasonry that Pike utilized in this degree to reinforce the principal that those who'd received the *Greater Mysteries* had a belief in reincarnation after their death.

The Letter *Aleph* Begins Five Semitic Alphabets

Phoenician   *Hebrew*   *Aramaic*   *Syriac*   *Arabic*

The practice of preparing for the journey to the next life is evident in the ancient Egyptian culture as well as others, such as the first Chinese Emperor Qin Shi Huang's thousands of terracotta horses and warriors, which were buried with him in 210 BCE to assist and protect him on his journey to the afterlife. Many contemporary academics espouse that the pyramids in Egypt were erected solely as burial chambers for their nobility; to protect them on their journey to the afterlife. It's clear from reading *Morals and Dogma* that the pyramids were constructed as a place to conduct the *Mysteries* in secrecy. It's easy to see how difficult the argument concerning the pyramids ultimate purpose was when all the hieroglyphics written about them was only readable by a minority of others in the population who'd also been initiated in the *Mysteries*; with their translation being lost to antiquity upon their civilizations decline.

The ancient Egyptians reserved the teaching and usage of hieroglyphics to only those who'd received the *Greater Mysteries*. John Fellows explains this point succinctly, "There appears also to have been a mixed language used by the priests, partaking at once of hieroglyphics and alphabetical characters; which, in allusion to the class of men by whom it was employed, was denounced hieratic. Hence, in process of time, the Egyptians found themselves in possession of three different modes of communication – the hieroglyphic, properly so called, the bieratic and the demotic or common." [60] The largest amount of the populace used the common demotic, however, nothing important from a historical perspective was written in it, as only hieroglyphics was used for such things. Because of this, the translation and understanding of hieroglyphics was completely lost after the decline of the Egyptian civilization.

The Egyptians recorded many important things about their civilization, culture and history, but they were of little value to historians until 1822. That was the year language prodigy Jean-François Champollion published the first complete translation of hieroglyphics, along with a grammatical reference. Until 1822, the discovery that both ideographic and phonetic signs were together essential for deciphering hieroglyphics had not yet been made. Champollion next published *Précis du Système Hiéroglyphique* in 1824, which became the essential work establishing the field of Egyptology, and, linked the later development of the Coptic language from hieroglyphs, while also assigning them phonetic values. The Egyptians strong observance of the duties of the *Greater Mysteries* allowed an entire civilization to record everything they felt compelled to document freely in hieroglyphics; without most people at the time, and, the entire world later being able to understand it. Keeping an entire written language secret, yet having it written everywhere for others to see for thousands of years is an impressive feat.

The masonic obligation shares the same commitment to fidelity that the priests and rulers of Egypt who had received the *Greater Mysteries* also held. This degree indirectly shows how fidelity and secrecy can successfully be maintained in perpetuity, or, for a very long time.

Pike summarizes well the overall purpose of this degree in its symbolic role as the *Greater Mysteries*, "The object of all the *Mysteries* was to inspire men with piety, and to console them in the miseries of life. That consolation, so afforded, was the hope of a happier future, and of passing, after death, to a state of eternal felicity." While reincarnation is again hinted at (with the hope of reaching eternal felicity upon death) the larger purpose of Freemasonry itself as a whole is momentarily revealed a few pages later in Pike's lecture, where he states, "It is easy to see what was the great object of initiation and the *Mysteries*; whose first and greatest fruit was, as all the ancients testify, to civilize savage hordes, to soften their ferocious manners, to introduce among them social intercourse, and lead them into a way of life more worthy of men." Civilizing society so that one may live freely while still observing the rule of law, and, continuing the education and wisdom of the liberal arts and sciences upon successive generations is the ultimate purpose of Freemasonry. Thus, the symbolic theme of Freemasonry is also so revealed; inspiring a just and tolerant civilization which both continues and thrives without its founders.

CHAPTER 20

NINE GREAT TRUTHS OF A TRINITARIAN

This chapter explores the twenty-sixth degree, which is called the Prince of Mercy; having previously been called the Scottish Trinitarian degree. Toleration and the concept of the holy trinity belonging to everyone are the lessons of this degree. This is the first degree in the Council of Kadosh that contemplates Christianity, and, the last of the Mystery degrees. In his rewrite of this degree, Pike used each of the Mystery degrees (the 23rd through 26th) to represent lessons from each major religious tradition history. This reinforces the idea that no religion has a preference or standing over another in Freemasonry; they're all equal interest and have something to educate each person without joining its ranks. The nine moral truths Pike exposes in the lecture at the end of this degree summarize the overall teachings of the Mystery degrees in the Council of Kadosh.

The final Mystery degree is a useful point to illustrate how each major religious tradition (at that time) is used in the allegory and theme of each of these degrees; reflecting the promotion of universal respect and toleration for the teachings of each. The comparisons below show these important distinctions.

Chief of the Tabernacle	**Eleusinian Mysteries**
Prince of the Tabernacle	**Egyptian Mysteries**
Knight of the Brazen Serpent	**Islam**
Prince of Mercy	**Christianity**

Where the Eleusinian *Mysteries* originated is not known. It's supposed they came from India, by the way of Chaldæa, into Egypt, and then carried into Greece. Pike states in *Morals and Dogma* that, "they were practiced among all the ancient nations; and, as was usual, the Thracians, Cretans, and Athenians each claimed the honor of invention, and each insisted that they had borrowed nothing from any other people." In Pike's words, the Egyptian *Mysteries* included, "All the ideas of the Priests of Hindustan, Persia, Syria, Arabia, Chaldæa and Phœnicia, which were known to the Egyptian priests and formed the primitive philosophy of Pythagoras and Plato." The origins of Christianity are more varied than Islam, however, contemporary audiences more readily understand both.

In the jazz musical style, each musician in the combo, quartet or band typically takes their own "turn" soloing during each song with their instrument. Most musical styles don't exhibit this egalitarian performance approach and seldom do many practitioners of modern religion; they tend to enjoy their attention in the spotlight, while ignoring the rest of the other performers. The lesson learned is that no religion is better than another. Each of them has important lessons to offer; these faiths often share more similarities than differences in the philosophical tradition. Too often we witness the despair or shunning of one faith by a practitioner of another in the name of God, which directly opposes the principles of divinity.

Pike writes a brief synopsis (a rarity given his long-winded writing style, which mimics deep thought) in *Morals and Dogma*, which summarizes the point of studying the world's religions for lessons that can be applied to everyone, regardless of creed or faith. "We do not undervalue the importance of any Truth. We utter no word that can be deemed irreverent by any one of any faith. We do not tell the Moslem that it is only important for him to believe that there is but one God, and wholly unessential whether Mahomet was His prophet. We do not tell the Hebrew that the Messiah whom he expects was born in Bethlehem nearly two thousand years ago; and that he is a heretic because he will not so believe. And as little do we tell the sincere Christian that Jesus of Nazareth was but a man like us, for His history but the unreal revival of an older legend. To do either is beyond our jurisdiction. Masonry, of no one age, belongs to all time; of no one religion, it finds its great truths in all. To every Mason, there is a GOD; ONE, Supreme, Infinite in *Goodness, Wisdom, Foresight, Justice* and *Benevolence*; Creator, Disposer, and Preserver of all things. How, or by what intermediates He creates and acts, and in what way He unfolds and manifests Himself, Masonry leaves to creeds and Religions to inquire."

The *Nine Great Truths of Masonry* are all grounded in morality and are represented in this degree by hangings in the lodge room (or stage) that feature alternating red and white columns, which is also used in the preceding ninth and thirteenth-degrees. A triangular altar sits in the center of the chapter room, with a white marble statue of a naked virgin, which represents truth.

An illustration showing an example of a naked virgin statue and a triangular altar is shown on the following page, along with nine corresponding truths defined by Pike in *Morals & Dogma*, taken from the chapter discussing this degree.

The Naked Virgin Statue of Truth

1. No man has seed God at any time; that is, God is only spiritual.

2. The soul of man is immortal.

3. The Moral Sense of man derives from God and therefore has a divine source and is a divine imperative.

4. Moral truths are as real as physical truths. They are not created by God but are a part of His nature; therefore, morality is not an arbitrary law of God but a part of that goodness which constitutes His essence.

5. The distinction between good and evil is essential. Having the ability to make the distinction is a unique quality of man whose

ability to do well is only made meaningful by his ability to do that which is not good.

6. There are no degrees in the practice of moral obligations; it's neither variable nor contingent. No excuse can justify one's failures to exercise the moral imperatives of a just life.

7. The immutable law of God requires, that besides respecting the absolute rights of others, and being just, we should do good, be charitable and obey the dictates of the generous and noble sentiments of the soul. We are but the almoners of God's riches and thus charity can know neither rule nor limit. It is the most sacred of all Masonic obligations.

8. The laws, which control and regulate the universe, are those of motion and harmony. Evil is merely apparent, and all is good and perfect. The existence of misfortune and adversity provides the opportunity for the expression of those virtues, which ennoble the soul and elevate the spirit of man; thus, is the evil of this world but part of the great plan of God for the betterment of man.

9. The last great truth of Masonry is the paradox of the equipoise of the infinite justice's infinite mercy of God; the former alone would call for man's utter destruction, the latter alone would permit the most offensive hedonism. Together they provide man with both retribution and forgiveness.

Perhaps the most concise and informative passage on the significance of Scottish Rite degrees in explaining the symbolic lodge rests in *Morals and Dogma*; the chapter for the Prince of Mercy degree explains the importance of the symbolism in the number three being used throughout Freemasonry. In addition to the *Nine Great Truths of Masonry* above, this passage is equally helpful for those looking to characterize the overall symbolism of the fraternity. "There are three Degrees in Blue Masonry; and in addition to the two words of two syllables each, embodying the binary, three of three syllables each.

There were three Grand Masters, the two Kings, and Khir-Om the Artificer. The candidate gains admission by three raps, and three raps call up the Brethren. There are three principal officers of the Lodge, three lights at the Altar, three gates of the Temple, all in the East, West, and South. The *three lights represent* the *Sun,* the *Moon,* and *Mercury; Osiris, Isis,* and *Horus;* the *Father,* the *Mother,* and the *Child; Wisdom, Strength,* and *Beauty; Hakamah, Binah,* and *Daath; Gedulah, Geburah,* and *Tepareth.* The candidate makes three circuits of the Lodge: there were three assassins of Khir-Om (Hiram Abif) and he was slain by three blows while seeking to escape by the three gates of the Temple. The excavation at his grave was repeated three times. There are three divisions of the Temple, and three, five, and seven Steps. A Master works with Chalk, Charcoal, and a vessel of Clay; there are three movable and three immovable jewels. The Triangle appears among the Symbols: the two parallel lines enclosing the circle are connected at top, as are the Columns *Jachin* and *Boaz*, symbolizing the *equilibrium* which explains the great *Mysteries of Nature*. This continual reproduction of the number three is not accidental, nor without a profound meaning: and we shall find the same repeated in all the Ancient philosophies." This passage is also an example of why Scottish Rite helps continue to build on the fundamentals of the symbolic lodge in the allegory and symbolism of its degrees.

The naming used for this degree has always been decidedly bizarre, with several other more relevant descriptions seeming more appropriate than Prince of Mercy, or, Scottish Trinitarian. The older name is more correct for its use of the word "Trinitarian" but given this degree takes place symbolically in a catacomb under Rome, the usage of the word

"Scottish" is questionable. Some more appropriate naming examples for the twenty-sixth degree are presented below.

Trinitarian of the Nine
Trinitarian Prince
Prince of the Trinity
Prince of the Faithful
Prince of the Nine Truths
Prince of the Triple Covenant
Initiate of the Faithful

Essentially, the *Nine Great Truths of Masonry* are all moral standards for life and can be faithfully followed by practitioners of any religion. While the trinity has a special focus for the Christian Mason, for example, the same lesson can be appreciated by one of another religion. All other religious practitioners are our equals amongst each other in divinity. The symbolic lodge requires a man to have a belief in a supreme being as a requirement for becoming a Mason, but does not stipulate any religion or tradition. Toleration requires the embracing of other faiths as being righteous and not discarding important teachings because they don't originate in the beholders holy book or scriptures. Thus, is the duty of a Prince of Mercy, or Scottish Trinitarian.

The lessons imparted in this degree can be realized in modern times with both positive and negative examples of organized religions cooperating. Simply consider some many examples you may remember of churches of different faiths rendering each other assistance. There's negative examples to ponder as well, such as the inability of the Muslim and Jewish faiths to collectively excavate the *Dome of the Rock*; so, the buried remains of the *Second Temple* can also be made available for worship side-by-side. The Scottish Trinitarian would defend the right of two faiths to worship in adjacent holy structures together in harmony and joy, working tirelessly towards such aims.

CHAPTER 21

KNIGHT OF THE BRAZEN SERPENT: THE ROD OF ASCLEPIUS

This chapter explores what the brazen serpent is, and, the symbolism behind the three different versions of this degree since it was first used by the Scottish Rite in the nineteenth century. This degree represents the most changed (or revised) degree ritual, both when Pike first rewrote it, and, when the current Southern Jurisdiction of the Scottish Rite in Washington D.C. revised it in 2000 as part of the *Revised Standard Pike Ritual.* This degree is the second most complicated amongst the Council of Kadosh degrees and the most recent revision in 2000 simplified it enough that the four main points can be covered now in under an hour. The degrees in this body are among the longest and as such, are difficult for many Scottish Rite valleys and orients to stage; the 2000 revision rectified this with the twenty-fifth degree, or Knight of the Brazen Serpent.

Numbers chapter 21 (of the *Old Testament, verses 6-9*) describes perfectly the legend concerning the use of a serpent in this degree. "And the Lord sent fiery serpents among the people, and they bit the people; and much people of Israel died. Therefore, the people came to Moses, and said, "We have sinned; for we have spoken against the Lord, and against thee: pray unto the Lord that he take away the serpents from us." And Moses prayed for the people. And the Lord said unto Moses, "Make thee a fiery serpent, and set it upon a pole: and it shall come to pass, that every one that is bitten, when he looketh upon it shall live." And Moshah made a serpent of brass, and put it upon a pole; and it came to pass, that if a serpent had bitten any man, when he beheld the serpent of brass, he lived." Fittingly, the jewel used for this degree is a golden Tau cross of the Crux Ansana of Egypt, which features an intertwined serpent. The Hebrew words *ytlx khalati* appear on the horizontal portion of the cross, meaning, "I have suffered." The vertical portion of the cross says *nakhushtan*, which means serpent, and, is generally regarded as a brass snake on a pole in the *Hebrew Bible*.

The Tau Cross

Moses with the Brazen Serpent

The current degree ritual states, "The Serpent was of old, among all peoples, a symbol of wisdom and of healing, and Christ charged his Disciples to be wise as serpents, and harmless as doves. Among the Druses, serpents have always been held in reverence. The Greeks called the Serpent *Agathodaimon*, the Good Deity or Genius; and the Basiliskos or Royal Serpent was a Symbol in Egypt. To us, the Brazen Serpent Nakhas, is a symbol of the wise interpretation which rescues the Divine Truths from the depravation which they have undergone by means of the ignorance of many interpreters, and the craft of more, whereby it is made easy for scoffers and infidels, by commenting on absurdities and corruptions, to bring all religion into contempt, making it appear the enemy of reason and common sense."

The symbolism used in each of the historical uses of the brazen serpent relate to the reverence typical of a philosophical (or moral) lesson in truth. The serpent imagery transcends religious faiths with a similar message; that those who stand freely before a deadly serpent and are bitten have nothing to worry about if they practice righteousness and truth. Rex Hutchens explains the connection Pike also makes in the degree ritual between the brazen serpent and the night sky, "The serpent in the night sky is called the constellation Scorpio and was thought by them to be along the path followed by souls in their descent to earth. So, the serpent became a symbol of malevolence; in the night sky Scorpio ushers in the period of darkness at the autumnal equinox. The serpent was also a symbol of eternity and immortality because in shedding its skin, it was thought to renew its youth." (Hutchens, 213)

While continuing the lecture of this degree, there's a passage that shouldn't be taken too literally, which says, "You are not to admit the authenticity of any passages taken from our Rituals and other Secret books, by one who is not of the Household of the Faithful, especially if he be of an illegitimate and spurious organization." Certainly, this doesn't mean that the authenticity of Scottish Rite degrees should not be freely communicated, discussed or taught. Too often in the history of Freemasonry has the confusion (or incorrect belief) existed that it's teachings must be kept secret and not discussed with non-Masons for free of reprisal, or, abandoning their obligations. Much of the degree rituals and other information is freely published; the civilized world benefits greatly when these teachings are handed down to successive generations, as Freemasonry is a progressive science; striving to educate society and not just the candidates for the degrees. Often, a sentence or statement is misinterpreted because of the original language style (not unlike Albert Pike) from when it was written not translating well to a modern reader, or, a desire to stress the importance of a given lesson being lost outside the literal symbolism of the degree ritual. This misconception is the special duty of brethren to ensure it doesn't occur in their Valley or Orient, and, amongst their peers, as it's also the duty of the casual reader (not involved in Freemasonry) to properly understand the context of the sometimes-complicated subject matter being presented.

Islam was chosen for this degree (or *Mohammedanism* as Pike called it throughout his degree rewrite) and it recreates the initiation rite of the Druse religious sect, who lived near present day Lebanon in 1450 AD. Pike radically rewrote this degree from the original version, which used familiar Hebrew characters instead; such as *Moses, Aaron* and *Joshua*. He spent a considerable amount of attention on this degree, writing the second most pages about it in *Morals and Dogma*, with only The Knight of the Sun degree being longer, and, more complicated.

It was then revised again and incorporated the Sufi (instead of the Druse) as part of *The Revised Standard Pike Ritual* in 2000, since the Sufi much better represented both the mysteries of Freemasonry and Islam. This degree was the most changed and was necessary because of Pike's error in using the Druse (during the rule of the Great Emir Sayeed Abdullah) as being representative of Islamic mystics. History suggests the Druse also held Gnostic and neo-Platonic views as part of their basic tenants, as well as being considered an abomination of Islam by Muslims living in the region then that's present-day Lebanon and

Syria. The Druse undoubtedly used some Islamic symbols, but simply weren't regarded as true Muslims by most people at the time.

The Sufi (practitioners of Sufism) considers themselves to be the original form of Islam. They further claim every order can trace its spiritual lineage back to the Twelve Imams, who were descendants of Mohammed. Thus, Ali Abi Talib is known as the father of Sufism. [61] Prominent orders still active today include the *Alevi, Bektashi, Mevlevi, Ba 'Alawiyya, Chishti, Rifa'i, Khalwati, Naqshbandi, Nimatullahi, Oveyssi, Qadiria Boutshishia, Qadiriyyah, Qalandariyya, Sarwari Qadiri, Shadhiliyya* and *Suhrawardiyya.* [62] Classical Sufi scholars have defined Sufism as "a science whose objective is the reparation of the heart and turning it away from all else but God." [63]

Pike was interested primarily in the symbolism of Islam for his rewriting of the degree ritual and it's possible that viewing some Druse symbols appearing Islamic was simply convincing enough. In the 1857 ritual, which is also known as *The Book of The Legenda*, Pike writes, "In many villages of the Anti-Libanus, the Druse inhabitants appear strictly to adhere to the tenets of Muslim law; being scrupulous in their attendance to rites and ceremonials, observing rigidly the Ramadan; but in this they only obey the precept of their own faith, which in secret they devoutly cherish." He continues (regarding his respect for the devotion) by saying, "The cities Ammatam and Bachlin are sacred to the Druses of Lebanon. They are rallying points, where, in times of trouble warfare, the tribes meet and swear allegiance to each other and to their cause, standing in their Khalue or Mosque, where all the books of their faith are guarded religiously and with jealous zeal." The spiritual devotion the Druse practiced, along with their use of rituals and symbolism, was undoubtedly why Pike chose them for this degree, giving it an Islamic theme.

What holds more controversy than the Druse being chosen as the group mimicked in this degree, however, is the identity of the earliest versions creator. The very first version of this degree (along with many others) bears the signature of Frederick the Great, who history agrees was a Freemason, however, most academics agree he did not supervise (or write) these degrees. Many regard the author of the *Grand Constitutions of 1786* to be anonymous thus, as no proof exposing any other authors has been successful. Given this degree has experienced the most revisions, it's instructive to consider this issue inside this degree's commentary; while it largely also mirrors the other Scottish Rite degrees as well, the chart below displays the chronological history of the degree revisions.

History of Brazen Serpent Degree Versions

1762, 1786	Frederick the Great	*Grand Constitutions of 1786*
1802	Estienne Morin	*Manifesto*
1855–1857	Albert Pike	*Magnum Opus*
1995–2000	Supreme Council, S.J.	*Revised Standard Pike Ritual*

Pike states in *Morals and Dogma* that, "This degree is both philosophical and moral. While it teaches the necessity of reformation as well as repentance, as a means of obtaining mercy and forgiveness, it is also devoted to an explanation of the symbols of Masonry; and especially to those which are connected with the ancient and universal legend, of which that of *Khir-Om Abi* (Hiram Abif) is but a variation; that legend which, representing a murder or a death, and a restoration to life, by a drama in which figure Osiris, Isis and Horus…and many another representative of the active and passive Powers of Nature, taught the Initiates in the *Mysteries* that the rule of Evil and Darkness is but temporary, and that that of Light and Good will be eternal." (Pike, 517) While Pike clearly integrated the symbolism and teachings of the symbolic lodge well in the other "higher degrees" he missed an important connection with the symbolism in this degree of a brazen serpent on a brass pole; this being a comparison with the Rod of Asclepius, the object of Greek mythology associated with healing or medical care in the present day. More surprisingly, this important connection and distinction was not incorporated into *The Revised Standard Pike Ritual* in 2000.

The Greek god Asclepius is associated with healing and medicinal arts, and, is symbolic of the healing temples built throughout Greece from 300 BCE onwards; such as the one on the island of Kos where Hippocrates is thought to have begun his medical career. Non-venomous serpents known as Asculapian snakes were used in healing rituals and were also placed on the floors where the sick were being cared for. The original *Hippocratic Oath* all physicians must take, for example, begins with the invocation "I swear by Apollo the Physician and by Asclepius and by Hygieia and Panacea and by all the gods..." [64] Pilgrims flocked to the Greek healing temples to make offerings and purify themselves before spending the night inside the holiest area. Dreams or visions were reported to a priest who then prescribed the appropriate therapy by a process of interpretation. Some healing temples also used sacred dogs to lick the wounds of the sick. It wasn't uncommon for a large quantity of Asculapian snakes to be introduced to any newly built temple.

The serpent and staff itself were separate symbols, which were combined during the development of an Asclepian cult. [65] The serpent is a symbol that unifies the duality of a physician's work, which deals with life and death, sickness and health. [66] The Greek philosopher Cornutus offers an excellent perspective on the integration of the snake and staff in his *Theologiae Graceae Compendium.* "Asclepius derived his name from healing soothingly and from deferring the withering that comes with death. For this reason, therefore, they give him a serpent as an attribute, indicating that those who avail themselves of medical science undergo a process like the serpent in that they, as it were, grow young again after illnesses and slough off old age; also, because the serpent is a sign of attention, much of which is required in medical treatments. The staff also seems to be a symbol of some similar thing. For by means of this it is set before our minds that unless we are supported by such inventions as these, in so far as falling continually into sickness is concerned, stumbling along we would fall even sooner than necessary." [67]

The symbol most people regard throughout the world as that of medical care (which transcends culture and languages) is the integrated rod and snake of Asclepius as shown below; note it's identical to the brazen serpent.

The Rod of Asclepius

This use of imagery throughout history is profoundly one of healing and medical assistance; be it during the time of Moses, the ancient Egyptians, Greeks, or, in the present day with urgent care signs illuminated with neon. This is the true meaning of the brazen serpent.

FURTHER READING

1. Arberry, A.J. *Sufism: An Account of the Mystics of Islam.* Routledge. 2013.

2. Baldick, Julian. *Mystical Islam: An Introduction to Sufism.* I.B.Tauris. 2012.

3. Bates, Victoria. Bleakley, Alan and Goodman, Sam. *Medicine, Health and the Arts: Approaches to the Medical Humanities.* Routledge. 2013.

4. Churchill, Charles, Henry. *Mount Lebanon: A Ten Year's Residence from 1842 to 1852 Describing the Manners, Customs, and Religion of its Inhabitants with a Full & Correct Account of the Druse Religion.* Garnet & Ithaca Press. 1994.

5. Cornutus, Lucius. *Theologiae Graceae Compendium.* Kessinger Publishing. 2010. (Reprint)

6. De Hoyos, Arturo and Morris, Brent, S. *Is it True What They Say About Freemasonry?* Government Institutes. 2010.

7. Green Nile. *Sufism: A Global History.* John Wiley & Sons. 2012.

8. Pike, Albert. *The Legenda and Readings of the Ancient and Accepted Scottish Rite of Freemasonry.* Kessinger Publishing. 2010. (Reprint)

9. Ridgeon, Lloyd. *The Cambridge Companion to Sufism.* Cambridge University Press. 2014.

10. Schimmel, Annemarie. *Mystical Dimensions of Islam.* North Carolina University Press. 1986.

11. Sherman, Edwin, Allen. *New Edition of the Brief History of the Ancient and Accepted Scottish Rite of Freemasonry: Together with a Historic Sketch of the So-called Revival of Freemasonry in 1717.* Carruth & Carruth. 1890.

CHAPTER 22

THE SYMBOLISM OF THE FIVE-POINTED STAR

The philosophical degrees of the Council of Kadosh present the use of the five-pointed star (or pentagram) and a rich amount of symbolism, which helps to understand both the wisdom and teachings of these degrees. The twenty seventh-degree continues the use of the pentagram in its symbolism, which was first introduced during the twenty-fourth degree, or Prince of the Tabernacle Degree. In this degree, it's represented prominently in the jewel used during the ritual, which is gold in color. It's most noticeable (overall) on the apron worn during the twenty-seventh degree, which reminds the viewer that it's a symbol of the microcosm, and, generally accepted as representing the five points of the human body. Michelangelo's popular sketches of the human body illustrate the points where the body intersects the pentagram well. The studious Mason may recall the *five points of fellowship*, which were first presented to them in the symbolic lodge, and, how they relate to this illustration of the human body against a pentagram. The sketches on the next page (from Heinrich Corneliusn Agrippas's *De Occulta Philosophia libri III*) were first published n 1531 and use the five-pointed star to symbolize astrology.

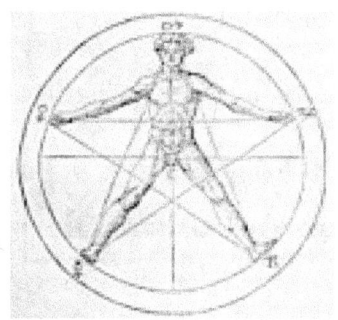 

To understand the symbolism of the pentagram in these degrees, it's helpful to have a basic understanding of how the symbol historically evolved. The word pentagram is derived from the Greek word πεντάγραμμον, which translates into "five lines." The first uses of the symbol were in Sumerian script and then next in Assyrian cuneiform. The word was used to describe a small room or opening and later evolved to mean "five corners" with some Assyrian variants using four corners instead. The Pythagoreans called the pentagram ὑγιεία, which translates as "health" and was also used as a sign of recognition. [68] Despite the confusing Assyrian variant of four, most of the world uses five to describe the number of sides on a pentagram.

The pentagram concept was developed on its own in Japan by Abe no Seimei during the tenth century, mostly for use on his family seal. He was a leading practitioner of *Onmyōdō*, an esoteric Japanese mixture of natural science and occultism. The pentagram is pronounced in Japanese as 五星 (or gobōsei) and is based on the Wu Xing (or 五行 in Chinese) or more commonly, as the "Five Elements."

The *Five Elements* came into maturity during the Han dynasty in China and may have inspired Abe no Seimei to incorporate the five-pointed star from Wu Xing into Onmyōdō. The *Five Elements* are Wood (木 *mù*), Fire (火 *huǒ*), Earth (土 *tǔ*), Metal (金 *jīn*) and Water (水 *shuǐ*) in Chinese. While this system lies at the core of acupuncture and other Chinese medicinal traditions and martial arts, it was also developed for understanding the relationships that exist among phenomena. The sequential order listed above in always used, which moves in a clockwise position. The interrelation between the *Five Elements* with both astrology and the natural sciences is not accidental and plays a crucial role in the overall symbolism of the Council of Kadosh degrees.

The pentagrams symbolic Eastern development is often recognized by the uninitiated as the "Ying and Yang" symbol, which is typically available as a logo just about everywhere on a variety of merchandise. Comparing the five-pointed star in Freemasonry with the *Five Elements* of Wu Xing (making essentially an Eastern vs. Western comparison) produces interesting parallels, which are more easily discernable by viewing them together, as the chart below illustrates.

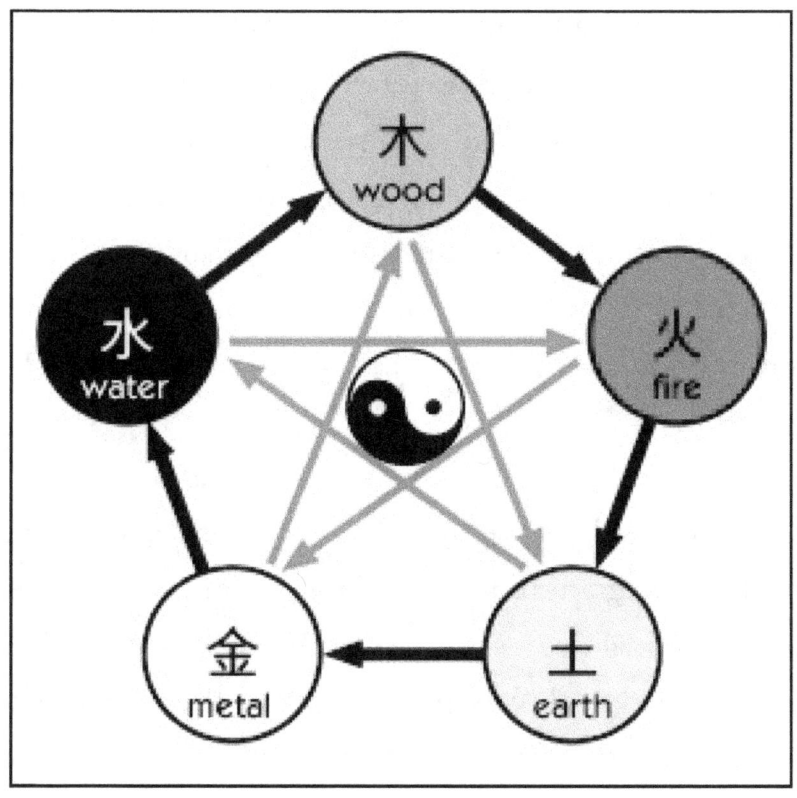

The pentagram was also used in ancient times as a Christian symbol for the five senses, which is also known as the five wounds of Jesus the Christ. [69] The fourteenth century poem *Sir Gawain and the Green Knight* describes the pentagram symbol prominently on Sir Gawain's shield; the unknown author credits its origin with King Solomon, explaining that each point represents a virtue that's tied to a group (or number) of five. It's said that Sir Gawain had excellent control of his five senses, was skillful with all five of his fingers, was faithful to the five wounds of Jesus, took courage from Mary's five joys of Jesus, and finally, that he exemplified the five virtues of knighthood. [70]

It's fitting that the Knight of the Sun, or Prince Adept degree is the final philosophical degree; the orders of knighthood begin with the next degree of Knight Commander of the Temple. Some of the preceding degrees in the Council of Kadosh have titles with "prince" and "knight" in them, but they're purely philosophical degrees. This is because they're using symbolism to explain ancient philosophical concepts and not because they're emulating orders of knighthood; this is a point of confusion to those not already familiar with the degrees, or, those who read the titles and only skim through a few pages of the ritual monitor, or, a few pages of Albert Pike's *Morals and Dogma*, for instance.

Once the philosophical degrees of the Council of Kadosh have concluded, the pentagram returns as a key part of the symbolism in the thirty-second and final degree, Master of the Royal Secret. The pentagram is featured in three separate degrees; the principal reason for this is the large number of symbolic themes it represents in Scottish

Rite Freemasonry. A reference to each of the three degrees utilizing the five-pointed star (and its main symbolic theme) is shown below:

24° *Prince of the Tabernacle*	**Alpha, Omega & Divinity of Man**
27° *Knight of the Sun*	**Symbol of the Microcosm**
32° *Master of the Royal Secret*	**Alura and the 4 Male Emanations**

The Prince of the Tabernacle degree initially exposes the candidate to the pentagram with an Alpha and Omega symbol in it. This is done because Alpha is the first letter of the Greek alphabet and Omega is the last. Using the first and last characters of an alphabet matters not in the language in which it's derived; the inherent symbolism is the beginning and end of all things, and, everything that lies in-between. The five-pointed star is presented with one point upwards intentionally in this degree as a symbol of the divinity in man. The final instruction concerning this symbol is its correlation to the five senses, five appendages (this degree counts the head as five; there's no additional arms or legs used in the ritual) and finally, the five fingers on each hand. The fingers together make up the two hands all Masons use for their various labors, which is a reminder that they should strive for perfection, so that the products of their labor may exist after them; hence a metaphorical beginning and end.

Next, the Knight of the Sun degree features the pentagram hanging in the west of the lodge room, revealing it as the sign of the Microcosm.

This can be characterized as the universe all sentient beings exist in. The pentagram symbol has long been considered a symbol of humanity because of the five outstretched points of a human body it represents. The apron for this degree has only a pentagram on it.

The third (and last) degree to use the pentagram is the Master of the Royal Secret, which is the last degree most Scottish Rite members receive in their lifetime. The pentagram represents *Ahura* and the four male Emanations. The first Emanation is *Ahura Mazda*. The second Emanation is *Spenta Mainyu*. The third Emanation is *Vohu-Mano* and the fourth, *Asha Khshathra*. *Ahura Mazda* was a Persian god of worship in Zoroastrianism, so it's fitting *ahura* means light and that *mazda* means wisdom. These relationships are illustrated below:

Ahura Mazda	Divine Might
Spenta Mainyu	Divine Wisdom
Vohu-Mano	Divine Word
Asha Khshathra	Divine Sovereignty

Every cross on the five-pointed star represents the four male Emanations. The candidate is reminded that when they received the Knight of the Sun degree, they learned the material and spiritual worlds are interconnected, which the pentagram also helps represent in the symbolism of this degree. Just as the thirty-second degree helps interconnect all the other degrees that precede it, the five-pointed star helps prepare the candidate to learn about the mysteries of the seven-pointed star and other interlocking triangles. The five-pointed star remains an important symbol in Scottish Rite, with no relation to the more sinister uses of the symbol by others outside the fraternity in the last century. To summarize, the five-pointed star can be described best in a single word as *humanity*.

CHAPTER 23

KNIGHT COMMANDER OF THE TEMPLE

Despite some of the titles used in previous degrees, the twenty eighth degree is the first of the three "chivalry degrees" which also conclude the Council of Kadosh. This chapter explores the history, purpose and theme of the Knight Commander of the Temple degree. The Crusades solidified the peak of chivalry and knighthood, as man's eternal struggle to avoid corruption, evil and temptation eventually saw the demise of chivalry. Literary knighthood examples, such as King Arthur and the Knights of the Round Table are the first many think of, however, the real Teutonic Knights (who assisted Christian pilgrims traveling to the Holy Land during the Crusades) comprised the historical *Order* of this degree's focus.

There were three levels of knighthood that were conferred historically; both in the mythical realm of King Arthur and the Knights of the Round Table, and, during the actual Crusades. Young men who desired to become apprentices to a knight would become a page, often at a young age. After some time, they'd become a squire after a special ceremony; only after more training and further service to the crown would one typically then be elevated to the title of knight. This accompanied a Christian-based ceremony, with the King presiding, which ended with the familiar crossing of the sword over the squires' shoulders, while in a kneeling position. Freemasonry's a progressive science; as such, the three levels of knighthood share parallels with the three degrees of the symbolic lodge, and, the three chivalric degrees of Scottish Rite, as shown on the following page.

PAGE	ENTERED APPRENTICE	*KNIGHT COMMANDER OF THE TEMPLE*
SQUIRE	FELLOWCRAFT	*SCOTTISH KNIGHT OF ST. ANDREW*
KNIGHT	MASTER MASON	*KNIGHT KADOSH*

In either levels or degrees except for the first, the initiate is expected to have learned all the lessons of the preceding degree, as well as improving the proficiencies of their craft; finding themselves deemed worthy and well qualified by their brethren to receive further light, or knowledge. The newly obligated knight, Master Mason or Knight Kadosh reaches the final level of chivalry in the same allegorical manner and shall likely never receive a higher namesake or honor. It's their duty to never miss an opportunity to assist, enlighten or educate others; most especially their brethren who seek their advice and counsel in confidence. The duty of receiving chivalric honor is the continued service for which it was awarded, with excellence and perpetuity; this is the ultimate lesson in the allegory of the chivalric degrees. The Master Mason and Knight Kadosh are no different, perfect or should otherwise be held in no higher esteem than those who've been conferred *Orders of Knighthood.* Each serves one common purpose under God; that is helping others and perpetuating the essential divinity and kindness of the human spirit.

The reception of this degree agrees with this assessment, "In order for this degree to be communicated, the Mason who desires to be honored and favored with it must have generally all the other Degrees, must possess the requisite qualities, and be provided with his titles, certificates, and briefs of reception, so as to prove by authentic evidence his regularity as a Mason...To be admitted to this Degree one must possess all the Degrees of Masonry, and thoroughly understand its principles, its bases, and its morality, in order to be able, knowingly, to decide in regards to matters that may arise even in the Lodges, among Masons." (De Hoyos, 707) While the standards of chivalry have remained somewhat high even in contemporary history, the changing world and increasing temptation of human weakness, coupled with a radical growth in the population of Europe were likely responsible for the overall demise of chivalry. In today's age, a man or young boy is considered chivalrous if they simply open a door for a lady; a far cry from the knights of the Order during the Crusades, who'd risk their lives to correct an injustice along their travels without so much as a thought about their own welfare.

In *A Bridge to Light*, Hutchens explains the purposes for the demise of chivalry and the importance of the ideals stated on the previous page, "…the age of knighthood came to an end as a result of human weaknesses—greed, political and religious corruption and, in general, the loss of the selfless attitude held by knights and demanded by the rules of chivalry. Despite the fate of knighthood, the chivalric ideal has survived as one of the noblest conceptions of the human spirit and provides the support for the ideals of family unity, moral education, honor and courtesy; all of which Masonry teaches as its duties." (Hutchens, 260) It's with the general cognizance of this fact that the duties of the Knight Commander degree are explained as being *devoted to honor, humanity, justice, loyalty* and *truth.*

Hutchens next discusses the history of the Teutonic Knights' creation, purpose and later demise, "During the Crusades groups of knights often banded together for common purposes such as to protect the travelers to the Holy Land or to reclaim Palestine from the Moslems for the benefit of Christianity. At the end of the Crusades in the Holy Land, the Teutonic Knights carried their crusade to Eastern Europe and conquered Prussia. This expanded their territory and influence. They were permitted by the Pope to engage directly in trading activities, despite their previous vows of poverty. The Orders expansion and increasing power arouse the hostility of neighboring countries, which join forces to finally defeat the Order. In 1466, a treaty entitled the Order to maintain some lands in Prussia but its Grand Master became a vassal of the Polish king. The complete disillusion of the Order began in 1525 when it's Grand Master converted to Protestantism and its lands reverted to Poland. Remnants of the Order, with scattered landholdings, existed until 1809 when Napoleon finely divided the land among other principalities." (Hutchens, 261) Frederick II authorized the Teutonic Knights to invade Prussia in 1236, which signaled the very beginning of later political resentment towards them. This story of a chivalrous Order being destroyed by engaging in successful trading shares a few unfortunate parallels with another chivalric Order, which is presented later in the thirtieth degree of Knight Kadosh.

Order of Teutonic Knights: A Timeline [71]

1198   The *Brethren of the German Hospital* are reconstituted as the *Order of Teutonic Knights*.

1199   Proclamation of the LIVONIAN CRUSADE.

1209   Teutonic Knights begin formulating their own customs.

1211   King Andrew II of Hungary grants the Teutonic Order all the Burzenland frontier.

1217–21   The Teutonic Knights take part in the FIFTH CRUSADE in Egypt.

1221   The Teutonic Knights are recognized as independent, international *Order of the Church*.

1225   Teutonic Knights are expelled from the Burzenland frontier, but invited to join the crusade in Prussia.

1228–29   The Teutonic Knights' conquest of Prussia begins.

1236   *Order of Sword Brethren* defeated by the Lithuanians.

1238   Abolition of the *Order of Sword Brethren* occurs; its members are invited to join the Teutonic Knights.

1283   Teutonic Knights complete their conquest of Prussia.

1309   Teutonic Knights move headquarters to Marienberg in Prussia, launching permanent Lithuanian pagan crusade.

1346   The Teutonic Knights complete the purchase of N. Estonia from the Danish king.

1398-99	The Teutonic Order joins with Lithuania to destroy the Golden Mongol Horde at Vorskla.
1410	The Teutonic Knights are defeated by Lithuania, Poland and their allies at Tannenberg.
1415-18	The *Council of Constance* debates the future of the Teutonic Knights.
1457	The Orders various estates in Prussia accept the Polish as overlords.
1483	The Teutonic Order loses its estates in southern Italy.
1492	The Teutonic Order loses its estates in Sicily.
1500	The Teutonic Knights lose their last possessions in Greece to the Ottoman Turks.
1501-2	Teutonic Knights of Livonia defeat Muscovite Russians.
1519-21	Teutonic Knights of Prussia are defeated by Poland.
1525	The Teutonic Knights adopt Protestant Christianity and secularize the Order in Prussia as a Polish fief.
1561-62	The secularization of the Teutonic Knights' territory in Livonia occurs, under Polish suzerainty.

The Teutonic Knights were founded in 1190 by Duke Frederick of Swabia and thrived until their military strengths demise started in 1525 when Grand Master Albert of Brandenburg resigned, converted to Lutheranism and then became the Duke of Prussia. [72] The Order would continue to survive however, with varying levels of autonomy from both other states and the Pope. They're known today as *The Teutonic Knights of St. Mary's Hospital in Jerusalem* and are based in Germany. They're motto's simply "*Help – Defend – Heal*" and they focus both on charity and ceremonial practices; not unlike other surviving Orders of the present day, such as the Knights Templar in the York Rite. The Teutonic Knights have an extensive history and were completely dissolved only once; this occurred temporarily between 1938-1945 because of being outlawed by Hitler. The black cross pattée image of the Order was used by the Kingdom of Prussia for their military decorations and then later, the Iron Cross decoration used by the German military. The black Teutonic cross remains in the Orders coat of arms and other images today; helping to explain and reveal the true origin of the Knight Commander of the Temple degrees "crossed column" logo, which is featured on both the apron and jewel. The picture on the next page shows the present–day coat of arms for the Order, which has featured the black cross pattée since 1190.

Honor, humanity, justice, loyalty and *truth* are values that have always been practiced by the various chivalric Orders and most certainly the Teutonic Knights; the Order this degree represents. The Knight Commander of the Temple is charged with being a champion to these essential causes in the present day, where a computer or telephone is used more than a sword. During the same time the Order was suffering during the Napoleonic Wars in 1802 and had signed the *Treaty of Amiens* (with its possessions and treasury being dispersed to neighboring German sovereigns) an early version of this degree was being worked in Charleston, South Carolina. Even as the Order was losing autonomy, it was still being honored for its history by Freemasonry and integrated into a new degree. In the reception portion of this degree, there's a passage that describes the early adoption of this degree in America, and, the esteem for which it was held. "The ritual of brother Louis Claude Henri de Montmain, who conferred it as a detached degree, in Charleston, from 1798 to 1802 and from when, in the former year Brother the Count Alexandre François Auguste de Grasse received it, says, "This sublime degree of grand Commander of the Temple Mason is the last, above all that precede it the most majestic, and the only one that has the greatest privileges; and it is for this reason it is styled the crowning point of Masonry, or the *NE PLUS ULTRA.*"" (Pike, 707) Whether the twenty-eighth degree is the most majestic is subjective and in the eye of the beholder; this quote however, echoes both the importance and respect that was afforded to a knight of the Order.

FURTHER READING

1. Ashbridge, Thomas. *The Crusades: The Authoritative History of the War for the Holy Land.* Ecco. 2011.

2. Hooper, Nicholas. *The Cambridge Illustrated Atlas of Warfare: The Middle Ages.* Cambridge University Press. 1996.

3. Kwiatkowski, Richard. *The Country That Refused to Die: The Story of the People of Poland.* Xilbris Corporation. 2016.

4. Mackey, Albert, Gallatin. *The History of Freemasonry: Its Legendary Origins.* Courier Dover Publications. 2012.

5. Morton, Nicholas. *Teutonic Knights in the Holy Land, 1190-1291.* Boydell Press. 2009.

6. Nicolle, David. *Teutonic Knight: 1190-1561 (Warrior).* Osprey Publishing. 2007.

7. Schmidt, Ferdinand-Karl. *The Occupation of Gotland by the Teutonic Knights, 1398-1408.* Loyola University of Chicago. 1966.

8. Smith-Riley, Jonathan. *The Knights Hospitaller in the Levant, C.1070-1309.* Palgrave Macmillan. 2012.

9. Stone, Daniel. *The Polish-Lithuanian State, 1386-1795, Volume 4.* University of Washington Press. 2001.

10. Turnbull, Stephen. *Tannenberg 1410: Disaster for the Teutonic Knights.* Osprey Publishing. 2013.

11. Urban, William. *Teutonic Knights: A Military History.* Greenhill Books. 2003.

12. Von Jeroschin, Nicolaus. *The Chronicle of Prussia: A History of the Teutonic Knights in Prussia, 1190-1331.* Ashgate Publishing, Ltd. 2010.

CHAPTER 24

SCOTTISH KNIGHT OF ST. ANDREW

When staged effectively, the twenty ninth degree of Scottish Knight of St. Andrew exhibits the most excitement and pageantry amongst all the Scottish Rite degrees; the wearing of kilts and the sounds of a bagpipe help bring this degree roaring to life theatrically. This chapter explores the important history behind the second of the chivalrous degrees, and, it's importance in Scottish Rite. Secondly, this chapter explores the modern day equivalent of the Knights of St. Andrew, as a service organization in some Scottish Rite Valleys; which lies under the oversight of the Master of Kadosh, or the senior officer of the Valleys Consistory. It's hoped this chapter will serve both purposes.

The cross of St. Andrew bears the symbolism in Scottish Rite of the nine essential qualities of a Knight of St. Andrew of Scotland. The virtues of chivalry are highlighted in this degree, and play an important part in the degree ritual. *Patience, humility and self-denial* are especially emblematic of the image of the cross and the holy persons who've unnecessarily died on it; these comprise the first three virtues. *Charity, generosity and clemency* are the next virtues, which also represent part of the obligation of a Knight of St. Andrew. Pike elaborates further in *Morals and Dogma*, "The Knights of St. Andrew vowed to defend all orphans, maidens, and widows of good family, and wherever they heard of murderers, robbers, or masterful thieves who oppressed the people, to bring them to the laws, to the best of their power." (Pike, 907) Sparing the conquered and the innocent are expected duties of a knight. The most famed men in the world have had in them both courage and compassion. [73]

The most important virtues of a knight are *virtue, truth and honor*, without which there'd exist no chivalry and no example of essential decency for an average person to aspire and follow in the world. A good example was published in 1858 concerning this subject, "Ye shall love God above all things, and be steadfast in the Faith," it was said to the Knights in their charge, "and ye shall be true unto your Sovereign Lord, and true unto your word and promise. Also, ye shall sit in no place where that any judgment should be given wrongfully against anybody, to your knowledge." [74] This degree teaches that virtue is a garment that's so sacred that even royalty wouldn't dare strike its wearer; further, that it's an allegorical suit of armor which protects one when unarmed, and, can only be lost if the wearer fails themselves. If one learns nothing else about chivalry in this degree, they'll still have grasped perhaps the most important concept; that the individuals have only themselves to blame if they lay virtue aside, speak lies, or, betray the honor of the knightly title bearing their name. The title of knight brings with it enormous responsibility and the requirement of serving others; it's not merely a respectful title to be used to seek the esteem, privileges or respect from others that it's insignia represents.

The x-shaped cross is emblematic of St. Andrew and the unfortunate crucifixion he suffered in the city of Patras, Greece (or Πάτρα, in modern Greek) at the hands of the Romans in 70 AD. Early religious texts, such as the *Acts of Andrew,* which was known to St. Gregory of Tours, describe St. Andrew as having instead been bound (and not nailed) to what's described as the same kind of Latin cross which Jesus had died upon. [75]   The tradition that developed which more people are aware of was that St. Andrew was crucified on an x-shaped cross (also called a saltire and known today as a St. Andrews Cross) at his own request; this was because he did not deem himself worthy enough to be crucified on the same type of cross in which Jesus the Christ had. [76]

Even if a saltire wasn't used, the image most people have of the patron saint of Scotland seems to show an x-shaped cross; this also is represented in the cross on Scotland's national flag, which has arguably made this theory far more popular. The x-shaped cross iconography, however, doesn't seem to have been standardized before the later Middle Ages. [77]   Rope was used to bind Andrew the Apostle's hands and legs, instead of nails.

This may have allowed St. Andrew to survive for the two days he spent preaching to the crowd from atop the cross, all of who were eventually converted by his words and demanded his release. (Elliot, 369) The Roman Proconsul Aegeas, whose wife had been baptized by Andrew the Apostle, eventually ordered that he be taken down from the cross; his men were supposedly then struck by a sudden and miraculous paralysis, which is thought to have been Gods response to Andrew's prayers that he might become a martyr. [78]

The legend concerning the Knights of St. Andrew in this degree's ritual owe their allegiance to St. Andrew the Apostle as the patron saint of Scotland, but also to King Hungus and his prayers for deliverance in the 8th century. Hungus' mixed Pictish and Scot force was completely surrounded by King Athelstan's English troops (who'd begun invading

Scotland in 934 AD) when he prayed to God and the Saints for help; the Apostle St. Andrew appeared before him and promised victory. The next day, Hungus' forces were indeed victorious and saw the image of the white saltire (representing the cross that St. Andrew had been crucified upon) against the brilliant blue sky. Thus, the origins of the Scottish flag, which remains the same to the present day, with its birthplace celebrated in Athelstaneford, a village in East Lothian, Scotland.

Pike elaborates further in *Morals and Dogma*, "…and Hungus and the Picts, after rendering thanks to the Apostle for their victory, and making their offerings with humble devotion, vowed that from thenceforth, as well they as their posterity, in time of war, would wear a cross of St. Andrew for their badge and cognizance." (Pike, 905) In terms of who was truly worthy of wearing the cross of St. Andrew, Pike discusses later in the chapter on this degree about the philosophical concept of "natural law" in choosing one's actions and to "let him who sees in great calamities the hand of God, be silent, and fear His judgments." Ultimately, however, Pike synthesizes the whole of men as having two natures in which to evaluate in determining those who might be admitted as knights, "There are two natures in man, the higher and the lower, the great and the mean, the noble and the ignoble; and he can and must, by his own voluntary act, identify himself with the one or with the other. *Freemasonry is continual effort to exalt the nobler nature over the ignoble, the spiritual over the material, and the divine in man over the human.* In this great effort and purpose the chivalric Degrees concur and co-operate with those that teach the magnificent lessons of morality and philosophy. *Magnanimity, mercy, clemency, a forgiving temper*, are virtues indispensable to the character of a perfect Knight." (Pike, 917) A perfect Knight is one who's worthy to wear the cross of St. Andrew; the ignoble Knight must perfect their practice of the *nine essential qualities*, in order that they may be judged worthy by their peers.

The *Grand Lodge of Scotland* adopted November 30 as *Saint Andrews Day*, and, the day for its *Annual Communication*. [79] Albert Mackey also noted that St. Andrew was held in high reverence not only by the Scotch, but also by the Russians and Swedish, and, that various orders of knighthood have been established in his name. Mackey later alludes to the origins of the degree ritual, "All of the high degrees he calls "Masonic reveries," excepting two, which he regards as containing the secret, the object, and the essence of Masonry, namely, the Scottish Knight of St. Andrew and the Knight of Palestine. The former of these degrees was composed by Tschoudy, and its ritual, which he bequeathed, with other manuscripts, to the Council of Knights of the East and West, was published in 1780, under the title *of Ecossais de Saint André, contenant le développement total de l' art royal de la Franche-Maconnerie*. Subsequently, on the organization of the *Ancient and Accepted Scottish Rite*, the degree was adopted as the Twentyninth of its series, and is considered as one of the most important and philosophic of the Scottish system. Its fabrication is, indeed, an evidence of the intellectual genius of its inventor." (Mackey, 806)

Unfortunately, most descriptions of the history of the Knights of St. Andrew all share the same brief, few paragraph description about their involvement in the crusades and their establishment in the city of Acre as the *Order of St. Andrew of Jerusalem*, and their historical records being lost in 1244 after being defeated by the Turks. Their role in guarding the Castle of Edinburgh for over 900 years is sometimes mentioned, but an explanation of the current form of the Knights of St. Andrew in modern Scottish Rite (as a service organization) is most of what's easily found. King Hungus' victory at Athelstane's Ford in Northumberland was followed by his barefoot troops then visiting the Kirk of St. Andrew to offer thanks to the Apostle and vow that both them and their future ranks would wear the figure of the St. Andrew's cross in both their banners and ensigns.

After a time, the services of the knights were not needed and many left the Order in pursuit of other affairs. Sir Levett Hanson's 1802 book *An Accurate Historical Account of all the Orders of Knighthood at Present Existing in Europe, by an Officer of the Chancery of the Equestrian Order of Saint Joachim*, states that it, "was not resumed till the reign of James VII, who created eight Knights, and for their better regulation signed a body of Statutes, and appointed the royal chapel at Holyrood House, to be the Chapel of this Order, as it still continues (and by his Direction it was repaired, having a fine Organ, with the Sovereign and Knights-brethren stalls, and their respective banners hung over them) but in 1688, the misfortunes of his reign preventing his completing that noble Design, it lay dormant till her late Majesty Queen Anne, was pleased to sign another body of Statutes, whereby it was restored to its "ancient magnificence."" [80]

Nisbet's Systems of Heraldry discusses the renewal of the Order by King James II (who was King of England and Ireland as James II and

King of Scotland as James VII) and its relation to the *Order of the Thistle*; an important distinction often missed. "In proof of this Order's being renewed by King James the Second, on the 6th of June 1687, and we are of that opinion; since we have seen, an original picture of the late Prince Charles-Edward Stuart, painted at Rome, in which he is represented, with the *Order of the Thistle*, as prescribed by the Statutes of King James the Second. It is not at all probable that this Prince would have so worn it, in consequence of the last renewal effectuated by Queen Anne, and which took place on the thirty first of December 1703." [81]

James V of Scotland was responsible, however, for the initial revival of the Order after its dissolution. "James the Fifth King of Scotland in 1554, received the *Order of the Golden Fleece* from the Emperor Charles the V, as also that of St. Michael from Francis I King of France in 1555, and that of the Garter in 1556. From Henry VIII King of England: and in Memory of These Orders received, keeping open the court, he solemnized the several feasts of St. Andrew, the Golden Fleece, St. Michael, and St. George of England: and that the several Princes "might know how much he honored their Orders, he set the Arms of the Princes (circled with their Orders) over the Gate of his Palace at Linlithgow, together with the *Order of St. Andrew.*"" [82] The third-degree lecture in the symbolic lodge discusses the nobility of the *Golden Fleece* and *Garter*; it refers to both these chivalrous orders and the esteem in which they're held meaning nothing if one cannot accept their obligations (and values as a Mason) and fails one's self.

Hanson elaborates further on the exclusivity of *The Order of the*

Thistle. "The *Order of the Thistle*, is of undoubted Antiquity, and is one of the most Noble in Europe. Save three Ribbons, which are reserved for a Prince of the Blood, and two English Noblemen, it is a national Decoration, which centers in a few of the opulent and powerful Families of Northern Britain. Since its revival in 1687, it has never been conferred upon any Nobleman under the Degree of an Earl; except in the Instance of the late Lord Viscount Stormont, (who was a Nephew to Lord Chief—Justice Mansfield) and upon the late Lord Cathcart; a Nobleman, who's Talents and Virtues were great and unblemished, and whose Abilities were ever exerted in the Service of the united Kingdoms. (Hanson, 16)

The correlation between the *Order of the Thistle* and the *Order of St. Andrew* is threefold. First, the patron saint of the *Order of the Thistle* is St. Andrew. Secondly, the *Order of Saint Andrew of the Thistle* is the full name of the Order; with it being simply called the *Order of the Thistle* now. Third, both Orders represent the chivalry and nobility of Scotland, with the *Order of St. Andrew* being prevalent during the early history of Scotland and the *Order of the Thistle* remaining active today. They complement each other in this fashion, however, the *Order of the Thistle* (as explained above) nearly always has selected members of nobility to be initiated into its ranks, whereas the *Order of St. Andrew* does not appear to have been as stringent of this requirement. Certainly, the Picts (some barefoot) who fought under King Hungus and saw **the white saltire of St. Andrew against the blue-sky overhead** (as depicted on the cover of this book) were not all the rank of Earl or higher! Lastly, Hanson informs us that the *Order of the Thistle* of Scotland was first instituted by King James V in 1540, but had gradually decayed instead of flourishing. (10) Between the years of 1540 and the revival in 1554, it's entirely probable that this decay may have been due (at least in some part) to the requirement of holding the rank of Earl or above; from a strictly mathematical standpoint. There are always more knights in a Kings army, for example, than merely Earls—or above in his court.

The legend of St. Andrew was not limited to Scotland, as discussed earlier in this chapter. The legend of St. Andrew had been transferred from Byzantium and adopted by Orthodox apologists for the rulers of Russia, who came increasingly to be identified as the founders of a new or "Third Rome." "Indeed, the growing imperial pretensions of Muscovite rulers from Ivan III on almost guaranteed that the Andrew legend would reappear in Russian political rhetoric. The foundation of the *Order of Saint Andrew*, the "First Called" (*Pervozvannyi*) at the court of Tsar Peter Alekseevich thus signaled the revival, in secular and chivalrous guise, of the ancient religious rivalry between the defenders of the Roman Catholic and Greek Orthodox imperial ideas." [83] The earliest records of its (informal) institution appear to indicate that the *Order of St. Andrew* was intended as an Eastern Orthodox counterpart to the Catholic knightly orders sponsored by the Holy Roman Emperor; most particularly to the crusading order of the seagoing *Knights of Malta*. [84] (It's worth noting that the *Knights of Malta* tradition is celebrated in the York Rite degrees in the present day)

The *Order of St. Andrew* is thought to have first existed in Russia in 1699 by the Tsar to reward those who'd distinguished themselves in battle against the Turks; during the Azoc campaigns between 1695-

1696, when Orthodox Muscovy was part of the *Catholic Holy Alliance*, consisting of the Holy Roman Empire, Venice, the Polish Republic, and the *Knights of Malta*. This was revealed in the diary of Johann Georg Korb, who was the secretary of the Habsburg ambassador to Moscow, who was a friend of F.A. Golovin (1650-1706) and who'd boasted of his membership in the new Order. [85] The name of the tsar's new *Order* however, appeared to have been borrowed from the earlier Catholic brotherhoods dedicated to St. Andrew; both the old Scottish Order known as the *Order of the Thistle* and the *Habsburg Order of the Fleece*, being originally dedicated to the Mother of God and Andrew the Apostle. (Boulton, 399)

Ziser notes that by founding Russia's first order of chivalry, the existing Cross of Constantine was then transformed into the Cruz Decussata of St. Andrew; this invoked the patron saint's protection of sailors in the Russian navy and other imperial ambitions of the tsar. (Ziser, 91) He elaborates further, "Both the honor and the burden of the tsar's personal trust in these men was embodied in the order's badge, a representation of the crucified St. Andrew in the form of the characteristic diagonal cross, which was worn around the neck on a sash or chain. By accepting the *Order of St. Andrew*, the men empowered to act as Peter's personal representatives on the stage of world politics took on the responsibility of fulfilling the words of the order's motto, "*For Faith and Fidelity*." Thus, like the courtiers who helped the tsar erect a cross in honor of the Pertominsk saints, the knights of the *Order of St. Andrew* were urged to take up the yoke of faith (*Acts 15:10-11*) and become the disciples of their royal patron and his heavenly intercessors." (Ziser, 93)

Regardless of which *Order of St. Andrew* is being referred, it's patron saint and commitment to fidelity of its members is the same. The biggest physical difference between the *Orders* seems to be their focus shifting from a military force to a chivalric honor society as time progressed; this trend has allowed for the (mostly) continuous existence of many other *Orders* from during the time of the various Crusades to the present day. A *Knight of St. Andrew, Knight Templar, Teutonic Knight*, or, *Knight of Malta* is more likely to be involved with charitable pursuits in the present day then taking up swords to protect pilgrims traveling to the Holy Land, etc. In honor of its origins and patron saint, the Scottish Rite Masons who have been deemed a Knight of St. Andrew do work for their local Valley. Helping the Valley with its day-to-day needs entitles those of the thirty-second degree to wear a kilt, glengarry, cock feathers and similar regalia to regular Scottish Rite functions and stated meetings.

The *Knights of St. Andrew* is a service organization with no central leadership or structure in Scottish Rite and is often referred to as KSA. The KSA has only one firm requirement, regardless of country or jurisdiction, the member must join as a thirty-second degree only; if a brother has attained the status of Knight Commander Court of Honor or the thirty-third degree, they cannot join, however, a member may continue to serve in KSA as an associate knight *after* being elevated to either honor. The only distinction being that they can no longer serve in a leadership role, such as Chieftain or Secretary, and, may not vote, however, they're entitled to wear a different colored cockfeather in their glengarry to identify this distinction. (See the next page for bonnet and feather insignia by rank) The KSA can formulate their own bylaws by chapter and serve under the direction of the Master of Kadosh. The Valley Secretary and Personal Representative often work with the Chieftain of the KSA chapter in getting items of an important nature resolved, but most especially with assistance in representing the Valley in public events (such as parades) and assisting with Degree Reunions, etc.

Acting as a greeter for stated meetings each month, special events throughout the year (such as the *Feast of Tishri*) and Degree Reunions by opening the door for arriving brethren is a simple, but valuable task that the officers of a Valley typically couldn't do at the same time, etc. The KSA acts as the glue and oil that keeps a Valley together and thriving. While the Degree Director is the ultimate authority, it is not uncommon for the KSA to stage and play a large role in performing and supporting the twenty-eighth, twenty-ninth and thirtieth degrees. The pageantry of the twenty-ninth degree is often a calling for those thirty-second-degree brethren who have the extra time each month to be active in their Valley's KSA. Not all Scottish Rite Valley's maintain a KSA chapter, however, they tend to flourish amongst the larger Valley's, in terms of overall membership; that's not to say that small Valley's do not have KSA chapters, however, the most active chapters tend to be in the larger Valley's. It's especially incumbent upon the officers of the Valley to consider the extra time and labor spent by the KSA chapter and help support them as needed, even if it's as simple as purchasing degree regalia, etc. The tradition of a knight wearing a sword is still honored in a ceremonial capacity, as brethren who dress in a glengarry and kilt will often carry a holstered sword on their shoulder or at the waist. The attention each KSA member affords to their regalia is also a means of honoring the Order and its earlier history.

Bonnet Badges and Feathers of the Knights of St. Andrew

Chieftain	3 Gold Feathers & Golden Bonnet Badge
1st Vice Chieftain	2 Gold Feathers & Golden Bonnet Badge
2nd Vice Chieftain	2 Gold Feathers & Golden Bonnet Badge
Secretary	2 Gold Feathers & Golden Bonnet Badge
Treasurer	2 Gold Feathers & Golden Bonnet Badge
All Membership	2 White Feathers & Silver Bonnet Badge

NOTE: *All feathers should be 6″ in length.*

SOURCE: www.KnightsofStAndrew.org

CHAPTER 25

COUNCIL OF KNIGHTS KADOSH

The thirtieth degree of Knight Kadosh is the third (and final) chivalric degree, and, the final degree of the Council of Kadosh in Scottish Rite. In the northern US jurisdiction, it's known instead as Grand Inspector. The use of history and symbolism of the Knights Templar (or *Poor Fellow Soldiers of Christ* and of the Temple of Solomon, or also as the *Order of the Temple*) make this degree an impressive conclusion to the "essential" degrees of Freemasonry. The lesson of this degree is "to be true to ourselves, to stand for what is right and just in our lives today. To believe in God, country and ourselves." [86] Tyranny still exists in society, despite "man being supreme over institutions and not they over him. He has natural empire and dominion over all things and institutions. They are for him not he for them. But the church, for profit and power, has reversed this natural law and order" [87] The theme of the degree ritual is well understood and discussed in other works, such as *The Scottish Rite Ritual Monitor & Guide*, but the original form of inaugurating officers each year for a Council of Kadosh is not, and, the principal focus of this chapter; along with a discussion of the Knights Templar's history and relevance in attempting to remove tyranny from the religious institution of the day, which lead to the day of Friday the thirteenth becoming unlucky whenever it appears on the calendar.

In the past, the yearly installation of Officers of each of the four respective bodies in Scottish Rite was conducted in closed session, and, typically at different times. (De Hoyos, 977) This made for additional ritual (since the body is opened on its highest degree) and in some cases, extra background on the degree's history was presented as well. In most Orients, today, the installation of Officers is performed as a single ceremony, which is open to the public and combines all four bodies together. This public version may be staged instead simply with authorization from the Sovereign Grand Inspector General, or deputy (which is usually the case) now. This is stated in Article XV, Section 13 of the *Supreme Council Statutes*, "The installation ceremony may, in addition, be performed either at a joint meeting or a joint and open meeting of Scottish Rite members, their families or friends, with approval of the Sovereign Grand Inspector General or Deputy of the Supreme Council." [88] While excellent for transparency and visibility in the community, and, nice to include the families and friends of incoming and outgoing officers, it detracts from the history and ritual, which could still be accomplished if the "closed form" session was also performed by bodies that could stage it without burden.

Pike felt that both the Council of Kadosh, and, the degree of Knight Kadosh were important enough to dedicate a short book for this purpose in 1879 entitled *Officers of Constitution and Inauguration of a Council of Knights Kadosh*, which is often overlooked by the new Scottish Rite brother or interested reader. After music and the Knights come to order, the Commander-elect makes a short address, followed by a brief discussion of the lessons or principles of the Knight Kadosh degree.

What occurs next is entirely appropriate for Knights Templar, but not something observed in the Scottish Rite degree rituals: the brethren

chant after taking their seats. This chant is provided in its entirety
below.

> *Blessed be the Lord*
> *God of Israel, because He*
> *Hath visited and wrought*
> *The redemption of His*
> *People.*
>
> *Salvation from our enemies,*
> *And from the hand*
> *of all who hate us.*
>
> *To perform mercy to*
> *Our fathers, and to remember*
> *His holy covenant.*
>
> *That being delivered*
> *From the hand of our*
> *enemies, we may serve*
> *Him without fear,*
> *In holiness and justice*
> *Before Him all our days.*
>
> *Blessed be the name*
> *Of the Lord, from hence-*
> *forth, now and forever.*
> *Amen!* [89]

Being a student of several languages and mirroring (again) that which
was practiced by the Knights Templar (or at a Roman Catholic mass)
Pike provides a Latin translation for alternative use:

> *Benedictus Dues Domi-*
> *Nus Israel, quia visitavit*
> *et fecit redemption ple-*
> *bis suae*
>
> *Salutem ex inimicis nos-*
> *tris et de manu omnium*
> *qui oderunt nos.*

Ad faciendam miseri-
cordiam cura patribus
nostris: et memorari tes-
tamenti sui sancti.

Ut sine timore de
manu inimicorum nostro-
rum, liberati serviamus
illi.

In sanctitate et justitia
Coram ipso, omnibus die-
bus nostris.

Sit nomen Domini be-
nedictum, ex hoc nune,
et usque in speculum.
Amen!

For the less intrepid council who doesn't wish to chant during installation, Pike then provides a song which can sang instead:

ODE.

The burden of the song we sing,
Serene or glad, shall preach to sorrow—
That sunshine follows after rain,
And after darkest night a morrow; —
That those who strive with evil days,
If their own strength they would but measure,
Might turn endurance into joy,
And outward woe to inward pleasure.

For earth, though filled with care and grief,
Has joy for those who wisely seek it;
And if the heart be truly taught,
It may defy the world to break it;
That Truth and Honor are not names,
But things, to those who prize them given;
And that the more we love our kind,
The more we make this earth like heaven.

The ceremony then proceeds like the beginning of the public installation at this point, with the Very Eminent Commander receiving the insignia of their office from the Master of Ceremonies; the difference being that the Master of each of the four bodies does this, since they're combined in the public installation. The Grand Chancellor displays printed officers' patents, the incoming Commander is asked if they wish to proceed; upon an affirmative answer, the following historical lecture on the Templars is read, the slightly edited words of which follow are important background there's simply no room to present in the Knight Kadosh degree ritual.

"*Fratres Militiae Sanctae Domûs Templi*, seven centuries and a half have passed away, since, in 1118, eight French noblemen, uniting themselves into a Society, became the Master and Brethren of the Temple. They first displayed the red cross upon the field, in 1148; were almost annihilated in storming Ascalon in 1153. The *Ball Omne Dotum Optimum* confirmed their principles in 1172 and they fought the great battle of Tiberias in 1187, the year the Holy City of Jerusalem surrendered to the Infidels. Other Crusades were preached, and the Soldiery of the Temple fought in the Holy Land until the end of the thirteenth century, by the side, in succession of Richard Lion-heart of England and Phillip Augustus of France, of Saint Louis and Edward Prince of Wales, at Damietta, Gaza and Acre, and, wherever a blow was to be struck for the Cross against the Crescent. On the thirteenth of October 1307, all the Templars in France were arrested; on the eleventh of March 1313, the Grand Master was burned. Princes had been members of the Order and its ambassadors had taken precedence of Christian kings. It had become too powerful by numbers, wealth and connections. It sought to be more powerful still by its influence upon opinions. In the East, the home of Gnosticism and where the doctrines of Saint John the apostle were still supreme, —in that Asia Minor of the seven churches, to whom Paul the new apostle contested the claims of Peter to the pontificate of the Gentile church, —in that Orient of which Patmos the apocalyptic isle was a part, the Templars had learned doctrines not acceptable to the Roman Bishops; it's probable that some of them had accepted those of Manes and were liable to the pains and penalties denounced against heretics. To the Monarchs of Christian, all of whom were at that day little more than the Deans of the nobility, maintaining a constant struggle against the ambition of their vassals; insecure in their places of power and without standing armies, the Soldiery of the Temple become a terror by their numbers, their immense possessions and their unity of organization. For the Order (had) dreamed of an Oriental Empire and sought to obtain by negotiation an eastern seaport. It was a standing army of proud, indomitable warriors, distributed all over Europe and obedient to the single will of the Grand Master. The Thrones and the Alters combined against it, and it fell and disappeared in a day. Its pride, ambitions and luxuries swelled the provocations that caused its ruin. During the centuries that followed, while it was merged into other *Orders* and wore the mask of Freemasonry, it was as is usual, chastened and purified by adversity. The advances made by science, the revival of letters, the reopening of the treasures of the ancient Grecian and Oriental wisdom, give it a deeper and sounder philosophical doctrine, and a wiser and truer religious creed. Its hereditary desire for vengeance on the despotisms to which its rein was due, were symbolized by the Mitre and the Crown, leading it eagerly to adopt the idea that governments are made for the people, and not the people for governments, upon its first announcement to the world." (Pike, 21)

After more esoteric discussion from Pike, we return to the lesson of this degree; that there's tyranny in this world, despite man supposedly being supreme over its institutions. "Society has no right to consider itself enlightened, while it regards the abuses of a system as its excellences, and makes idols of its own prejudices, and looks with horror on attempts to obtain rational reforms as revolutionary projects; nor while it continues to be ignorant that the criminal instincts are the most frightful of all the mental maladies, and does not comprehend that the diseased should be cured and not put to death, has it any right to consider itself Christian. Keep these truths always in view, in the warfare in which you are incessantly to wage against tyrannies. For there are not only tyrannies of Thrones and Pontificates, but also of the People and Parties, Opinion and of the Law. Close around you everywhere, you will find evils enough to combat; and it will be well for you if you do not become their ally." [90]

The discourse then continues. "The days have retired but a little way into the past, when men were divided into but two classes— the oppressor and the oppressed. Then Thought was imprisoned; to breathe it was peril, if not death, and it died in the brain where it was born, or was only whispered in the solitudes. The obligations of Blue Masonry are retained, that they may incessantly remind us of those wretched days. Now, Thought is as free as the wind and the lightning flashes it across the oceans and around the continents. Nations are enfranchised by it, and the golden glories of Truth begin to illuminate

162

the world. A new power has arisen among men, known as Public Opinion, with a new weapon, the Press. Before it, even the kings recede and yield to it and obey its Bulls and Allocutions, or it shakes down their thrones into the dust." (Chaplin, 387) After this much enlightening and timeless lecture, the brethren next join in song, as provided below:

> *We have a Holy House to build,*
> *A Temple splendid and divine,*
> *To be with glorious memories filled;*
> *Of Right and Truth to be the shrine.*
> *How shall we build it strong and fair, —*
> *This Holy House of Praise and Prayer,*
> *Firm-set and solid, grandly great! —*
> *How shall we all its rooms prepare*
> *For use, for ornament, for state?*
>
> *Our God hath given the wood and stone,*
> *And we must fashion them aright,*
> *Like those who toiled on Lebanon,*
> *Making the labor their delight:*
> *This House, this Palace, this God's House,*
> *This Temple with its lofty dome,*
> *Must be in all proportions fit,*
> *That heavenly messengers may come,*
> *To lodge with those who tenant it.*
> *Build squarely up the stately walls,*
> *The two symbolic columns raise,*
> *And let the lofty courts and halls*
> *With all their golden glories blaze,*
> *There, in the Kadosh-Kadoshira,*
> *Between the broad-winged cherubim,*
> *Where the Shekinah once abode,*
> *The heart shall raise its daily hymn*
> *Of gratitude and love to God.*

The oaths of office are taken next, in a manner like a combined public installation; music and chanting continue once again before the council proceeds to close. The unique insight of this ceremony highlights not only the lesson of man resisting tyranny, which exists in the Knight Kadosh degree ritual, but also a history and insight into the Knights Templar and their practices. An example of an average Templar day [91] is outlined in the following chart.

Templar Day Per the Rule of the Temple

TIME	ACTIVITY	SERVICE TYPE
NIGHT	Matins in Chapel	Brothers to join in prayers, then check horses and equipment and speak to squires. Sleep until dawn.
6:00 AM	Prime Mass	
9:00 AM	Terse	
12:00 PM	Sext Mass	Repair armor and equipment; make tent pegs, posts, etc. Followed by lunch, with Knights at 1st sitting, Sergeants at 2nd and the clerk reading aloud while all eat. Give thanks in chapel: *"Go to their posts and do the best that God instructs them."*
3:00 PM	Nones, Vespers, Vigils	
DUSK	Vespers	Followed by supper.
DUSK	Compline	Followed by a drink. Check horses and equipment, speak to squire, if necessary.
DARK	None	Bed.

For historical authenticity, Pike provides a listing of Knight Templar names for Valley's to consider using in naming their Council of Kadosh. This list is provided for reference on the following page. In the French language, the "de" in each last name is typically used to indicate where the person hailed from, or, their family's nobility, and is known as a nobiliary particle; not all using it are of nobility, however.

Suggested Names for Councils of Kadosh

ALAN DE NEVILLE
AMENT DE ST. MAUR
ARCHAMBAUD SE ST. AGNAN

ARNOLD DE TOUR ROUGE
BALDWYNE DE FLANDERS
BALIAN D'IBELIN
BERNARD DE TREMELAY
BERTRAND DE BLANQUEPORT

EUDES DE SAINT AMANT
EVERBARD DES BARRES
GEOFFROI BISOL
GEOFFROY DE SAINT-ADEMA

GERARD DE RIDERFORT
GILBERT DE LACY
GUY DE CREON
GUY DE LUSIGNAN
HERMAN DE PERIGORD
HUGH DE NEVILLE
HUGUES DES PAYENS
INGRAM DE BRUCE
JACQUELINE DE MAILLY
JOHN DE DEUX
JOHN DE LACY

ODO DE ST. AMAND
PAYEN DE MONTDIDIER
PHILIPPE DE NAPLOUS

PHILIPPE DU PLESSEIS
PIERRE DE MONTAIGU
REGINALD DE ARGENTINE
RICHARD DE CLARE
ROBERT BRUCE OF ANNAN

ROBERT DE CRAON
ROBERT DE SABLE
ROBERT DE SANDFORD
ROBERT FRITZ PARNELL

WALTER DE BEAUCHAMP
WALTER DE CLIFTON
WALTER DU MESNIL
WILLIAM DE BEAUJEU
WILLIAM DE CHARTRES
WILLIAM DE CRESPIGNY
WILLIAM DE LA MORE
WILLIAM DE MONTFERRAT
WILLIAM DE ROCHEFORT
WILLIAM DE SANDFORD
WILLIAM DE SONNAC

SOURCE: *Officers of Constitution & Inauguration off Knights Kadosh*

Finally, it's instructive to consider the timeline of the Templars; a chivalric Order beginning in 1120 which thrived in many countries and was shamefully dismantled in 1312, with many of its knights brutally executed (or tortured in prison) at the behest of the Pope, who feared their monetary and political influence. An Order that only existed for 192 years still managed to fight in an impressive 11 crusades and generate much historical interest. A chart including the Templar chronology is provided below, with portions taken from the book *Knight Templar 1120-1312*.

Templar Chronology

1095   Pope Urban II calls for the FIRST CRUSADE.

1099   The FIRST CRUSADE captures Jerusalem and the kingdom of Jerusalem is established.

1129   The *Order of the Temple* gets papal approval during *Council of Troyes* in France.

1136-7   Templars are established in *Amanas March*, north of Antioch in Syria. (which is now Turkey)

1147-9   SECOND CRUSADE.

1187   Saladin captures Jerusalem in the *Battle of Hattin*, executing all the Templar prisoners.

1189-2   THIRD CRUSADE.

1191   Templars establish new headquarters at *Acre*. (which is now *Akko* in Israel)

1204   FOURTH CRUSADE captures Constantinople.

1216   Intermittent war ends with King Leon over the *Amanus March*.

1217   FIFTH CRUSADE occurs in Egypt and Palestine until 1221.

1228-9 CRUSADE OF FREDERICK II. Jerusalem is recovered but the Temple Mount is not.

1239 CRUSADE OF THEOBALD OF CHAMPAGNE AND NAVARRE lasts for one year.

1240-1 CRUSADE OF EARL RICHARD OF CORNWALL.

1248 CRUSADE OF LOUIS IX OF FRANCE. This crusade occurred in Egypt & Palestine until 1254.

1270 LOUIS IX'S SECOND CRUSADE to Tunis occurs.

1271-2 CRUSADE OF THE LORD EDWARD OF ENGLAND.

1274 The *Second Council of Lyons* discusses a new crusade, which never begins.

1289 Sultan Qalawun of Egypt captures Tripoli. (which is now *Tarabalus* in Syria)

1291 Templars excavate Castle Pilgrim, Sidon and Tortosa, before moving their headquarters to Cyprus.

1302 Templars lose Ruad Island to Sultan Al-Malik, al-Nasir Mohammad of Egypt.

1306 King Henry II of Cyprus is ousted by his brother, who the Templars supported.

1307 The Templars in France are arrested on the orders of King Phillip IV.

1310 King Henry II returns to power, putting the Templars under arrest.

1311-2   Church council held at Vienne in France.

1312   Pope Clement IV abolishes Templars, gives their property to the Hospitallers.

1314   James of Molay and Geoffrey of Charney are burned to the stake in Paris.

1316-7   Ayme d'Oselier and other Templars from Cyprus die in prison.

1319   The *Order of Montesa* is established in the kingdom of Valencia, receiving former *Order of the Temple* property. The *Order of Christ* is established in Portugal with former *Order of the Temple* property.

CHAPTER 26

THE SUPREME TRIBUNAL

Despite being one of only two degrees in the Consistory, and, one of the more interesting degree rituals in Scottish Rite (delving into the Hall of Judgment in the Egyptian Court of the Dead) the thirty-first degree of Inspector Inquisitor is perhaps the least worked degree of all. The officers of the Consistory typically only confer the next degree in most orients; whereas the officers in the other three bodies always have more degrees to work, by default. The jewel of this degree is the Teutonic cross, suspended from a chain, which symbolizes each of the eight fundamental degrees of Freemasonry; the three symbolic degrees, the Secret Master, Perfect Elu, Prince of Jerusalem, Knight Rose Croix and Knight Kadosh. This chapter focuses on the Egyptian supreme tribunal in this degree's ritual and the judgment of each recently deceased soul for rendering passage to the afterlife, or kingdom of the gods. Pike summarizes the purpose of this degree is to learn to judge impartially, "To hear patiently, to weigh deliberately and dispassionately, and to decide impartially; —these are the chief duties of a Judge." (Pike, 935)

The *Book of the Dead* was an ancient funerary text, which was principally used between 1550 and 50 BCE. [92] The original Egyptian name for the book, transliterated "*rw nw prt m hrw*" means literally *Book of Coming Forth by Day*. [93] No single version existed, as this book was made up of several spells from Egyptian history and earlier works, such as the Coffin and Pyramid Texts, which spanned 1,000 years of written versions. The book was designed to assist in preparing for the journey through the afterlife after death. After all the obstacles of preservation and the afterlife transition (called the *Duet*) were completed, the judgment process began. This is what the degree ritual is necessarily concerned with, hence the use of supreme tribunal.

The "Weighing of the Heart" ritual, which has traditionally been identified as Spell 125, was utilized during judgment. The deceased soul was brought before Osiris by the god Anubis, where they were caused to swear they hadn't committed any of several forty-two different sins during their lifetime. (Taylor, 135) This astonishing number of sins (many of which are heavily subjective) is listed (mostly unabridged) below.

I have not committed sin.
I have not committed robbery with violence.
I have not stolen.
I have not slain men and women.
I have not stolen grain.
I have not purloined offerings.
I have not stolen the property of the gods.
I have not uttered lies.
I have not carried away food.
I have not uttered curses.
I have not committed adultery; I have not lain with men.
I have made none to weep.
I have not eaten the heart [i.e., Not grieving uselessly].
I have not attacked any man.
I am not a man of deceit.
I have not stolen cultivated land.
I have not been an eavesdropper.
I have slandered [no man].
I have not been angry without just cause.
I have not debauched the wife of any man.
I have not debauched the wife of [any] man.

(Repeats the previous, but addressed to a different God)

I have not polluted myself.
I have terrorized none.
I have not transgressed [the Law].
I have not been wroth.
I have not shut my ears to the words of truth.
I have not blasphemed.
I am not a man of violence.
I am not a stirrer up of strife (or a disturber of the peace).
I have not acted (or judged) with undue haste.
I have not pried into matters.
I have not multiplied my words in speaking.
I have wronged none, I have done no evil.
I have not worked witchcraft against the King.
I have never stopped [the flow of] water.
I have never raised my voice (spoken arrogantly, or in anger).
I have not cursed (or blasphemed) God.
I have not acted with evil rage.
I have not stolen the bread of the gods.
I have not carried away the *khenfu* cakes from the dead spirits.
I have not snatched away the bread of the child, nor treated with
      contempt the god of my city.
I have not slain the cattle belonging to the God. [94]

As one can see, this exhaustive list is one not many persons could honestly negotiate; the degree ritual fortunately does not ask the candidate forty-two questions about their potential sins.

After the list of sins, or "the Negative Confession" had ben read, and, the dead had responded, the goddess Ma 'at would weigh their heart using a scale; if the deceased had led a virtuous-enough life, the scales would balance. If they had not, the scales would of course, not balance. In the *Book of the Dead*, the use of Spell 30B by the practitioner was thought to help protect them during the weighing process. Anubis would conduct the deceased who passed the test of Ma'a'ts scales to

Osiris, to find their place in the afterlife and become *maa-kheru*, which means, "vindicated" or "true of voice." (Taylor, 215) If the scales didn't balance, a fearsome beast called Ammit the Devourer was ready to eat their heart and bring the dead person's afterlife to both an early and unpleasant end. (Taylor, 212)

Ogden Goelet, a well-known Egyptian language and culture professor at *New York University*, points out that, "Without an exemplary and moral existence, there was no hope for a successful afterlife." [95] In contrast to this, Geraldine Pinch suggests that the "Negative Confession" is no different than the spells protecting from demons, and, that the success of the "Weighing of the Heart" ritual depended on the mystical knowledge of the true names of the judges rather than on the deceased's moral behavior. [96]

The use of such rituals was meant more as the example for the living to be mindful of, as opposed to simply their instruction book for the afterlife. "We must understand that such descriptions were not intended to simply justify the progress of the deceased beyond the tomb but to caution the living about their future. The "deceased" in the *Mysteries* should be recognized as one who would live simultaneously in the world of the beyond and the world of the now, seeing the reality behind the shadow world of matter. He was not merely one who had his consciousness snuffed out and then recreated in the afterlife. Rather, it would have been more applicable to someone who had the courage to plunge into the *Mysteries*, face the darkness, uncertainties, and terrors of the other world, and then emerge into the light of day as another force, another radiance, participating in the stream of cosmic consciousness." [97] Hence, the use of the teachings to reinforce the moral law of justice amongst the living population; this is a central theme for Pike's discussion about this degree, along with the problems of temptation.

The moral law of justice is what the *Court of the Dead* was essentially trying to seek in whether a candidate for the afterlife had followed. The list of forty-two sins was the ancient Egyptians attempt at differentiating this normative principal with an empirical basis, making the difficult principles of justice easier to navigate and understand. Pike doesn't explain this nuance in *Morals and Dogma*, but offers the following thoughts on the moral law of justice. "It is not only true that we may learn the moral law of justice, the law of right, by experience and observation; but that God has given us a moral faculty, our conscience, which is able to perceive this law directly and immediately, by intuitive perception of it; and it is true that man has in his nature a rule of conduct higher than what he has ever yet come up to, —an ideal of nature that shames his actual of history: because man has ever been prone to make necessity, his own necessity, the necessities of society, a plea for injustice. But this notion must not be pushed too far—for if we substitute this ideality for actuality, then it is equally true that we have within us an ideal rule of right and wrong, to which God Himself in His government of the world has never come, and against which He (we say it reverentially) every day offends." (Pike, 941) The Grand Archivist and Grand Historian of Scottish Rite at the *House of the Temple* explained to the author that the reason for this is because *Morals and Dogma* was published before the Egyptian theme was introduced into the thirty-first degree.

The conception of morally right versus wrong is also espoused by Pike, who seemed to posit a "natural law" approach to his writing on justice; natural law is a system of law that's determined by nature and hence universal. [98] "It is entirely true to say that justice is the constitution or fundamental law of the moral Universe, the law of right, a rule of conduct for man (as it is for every other living creature), in all his moral relations. No doubt all human affairs (like all other affairs), must be subject to that as the law paramount; and what is right agrees therewith and stands, while what is wrong conflicts with it and falls. The difficulty is that we ever erect our notions of what is right and just into the law of justice, and insist that God shall adopt that as His law; instead of striving to learn by observation and reflection what His law is, and then believing that law to be consistent with His infinite justice, whether it corresponds with our limited notion of justice, or does not so correspond. We are too wise in our own conceit, and ever strive to enact our own little notions into the Universal Laws of God." (Pike, 939)

Despite our very best efforts, it's simply not possible for the individual, or the society to uphold the ideals of justice all the time. "The ideal justice which men ever look up to and strive to rise toward, is true; but it will not be realized in this world." (Pike, 943) In striving to avoid poor judgment amid human nature to err, Pike offers the following thought concerning others' opinions of us from the aggregate of our mistakes over correct actions. "Injustice, public or private, like every other sin and wrong, is inevitably followed by its consequences. The selfish, the grasping, the inhuman, the fraudulently unjust, the ungenerous employer, and the cruel master, are detested by the great popular heart; while the kind master, the liberal employer, the generous, the humane, and the just have the good opinion of all men, and even envy is a tribute to their virtues." (Pike, 944)

After discussing the moral law of justice that's depicted in the degree ritual and in this degree's chapter in *Morals and Dogma*, Pike reminds the reader about the other responsibilities inherent to an Inspector Inquisitor. "Remember also, my Brother, that you have other duties to perform than those of a judge. You are to inquire into and scrutinize carefully the work of the subordinate Bodies in Masonry. You are to see that recipients of the higher Degrees are not unnecessarily multiplied; that improper persons are carefully excluded from membership, and that in their life and conversation Masons bear testimony to the excellence of our doctrines and the incalculable value of the institution itself. You are to inquire also into your own heart and conduct, and keep careful watch over yourself, that you go not astray. If you harbor ill-will and jealousy, if you are hospitable to intolerance and bigotry, and churlish to gentleness and kind affections, opening wide your heart to one and closing its portals to the other, it is time for you to set in order your own temple, or else you wear in vain the name and insignia of a Mason, while yet uninvested with the Masonic nature." (Pike, 937)

The degree ritual has similar guidance for the candidate. "Ever remember that, being human, you must of necessity often err; that those who hold different opinions entertain them as honestly as you do your own: and that you have no right to deny or doubt their sincerity. Especially, never harshly denounce an opinion that more experience and a more thorough investigation may someday compel you to adopt, and therefore always treat your opponents as if their opinions were at some time to become your own. No man is truly wise who is not kind and courteous, charitable in his construction of men's motives, lenient and distrustful of his own ability to resist the allurements of temptation, and afraid of the mighty influences of prejudice and passion. Remember that you represent the Order; that you must maintain its dignity and glory, preserver it's Constitutions, and act by its laws. You are ever to bear in mind that what the letter of the law does not prohibit, is often forbidden by generosity and decency." (De Hoyos, 810)

Osiris personifies the overall lesson of this degree in the degree ritual as part of his spoken dialogue. "The strong who easily resist temptation are less deserving than the weak who struggle to overcome. To fall and rise again is more heroic than by greater strength never to fall. To do wrong, and make amends, to sin and to repent belong to a noble nature. The gods love man the more, because they are not perfect, even as fathers love their children, with their weaknesses and faults. (De Hoyos, 810) To this point, it's instructive to not obsess about our past failures of judgment and instead focus on not repeating them, while similarly offering wise counsel to those who may use it; so, they might avoid themselves making a poor judgment, since temptation is indelibly part of human nature.

FURTHER READING

1. Assman, Jan. *Death and Salvation in Ancient Egypt.* Cornell University Press. 2005.

2. Budge, E.A. Wallis. *Osiris and the Egyptian Resurrection.* Courier Corporation. 2012.

3. Budge, E.A. Wallis. *The Egyptian Book of the Dead: The Papyrus of Ani in the British Museum.* Cosimo Inc. 2010.

4. Mancini, Anna. *Maat Revealed, Philosophy of Justice in Ancient Egypt.* Buenos Books America LLC. 2004.

5. Morenz, Siegfried. *Egyptian Religion.* Cornell University Press. 1992.

6. Pincg, Geraldine. *Egyptian Mythology: A Guide to the Gods, Goddesses, and Traditions of Ancient Egypt.* Oxford University Press. 2002.

7. Ray, John. *Reflections of Osiris: Lives from Ancient Egypt.* Oxford University Press. 2002.

8. Schafik, Allam. *Ma 'at – Justice and Immortality in Ancient Egypt; Und: Books and Libraries in Ancient Egypt.* Wissenschaftliche Verlagsgesellschaft. 1991.

9. VerSteeg, Russ. *Law in Ancient Egypt.* Carolina Academic Press. 2002.

10. Wendrich, Willeki. *Egyptian Archaeology.* John Wiley & Sons. 2011.

CHAPTER 27

PRINCE OF THE ROYAL SECRET

Despite both the degree ritual and Pike's chapter on it in *Morals and Dogma* being too long, the thirty-second and final degree in the Consistory has an impressive pageantry with the revealing of the *Masonic Camp* and a summation of the larger points of each of the four bodies in Scottish Rite. This degree is the unification of all the rest; revealing the royal secret to be *equilibrium*. This chapter focuses on the symbolism of the star in the ritual, and, the importance of continuing a civilized and just society; which respects both the rule of law and peaceful democratic autonomy for the individual. Masonry is a beckoning light towards freedom, but Scottish Rite expands on this concept further, using allegory and symbolism to explain the responsibility of those who recognize its ideals to necessarily enforce them against the likes of injustice and tyranny.

The *Masonic Camp* is the first illustration of complete symbolism presented in Scottish Rite. All twenty-eight degrees are presented in an intentional sequence, with the importance and necessary interrelation of their lessons revealed as well; a complete blueprint for a civilized and just society, which respects liberty. The greater secret lies not within *equilibrium*, or balance amongst all things, but that this degree also uses empirical standards to prove the wisdom of the normative logic which was so prevalent amongst the Gnostics and philosophers such as Plato. The concept of a just and orderly society with liberty is reinforced with the numbers presented in the lights, the Tetractys and other groupings discovered within the symbolism of each degree. The thirty-second degree serves no purpose but to explain all those preceding it, and, to reveal the wisdom of its organization and structure.

Early Floor Model Depicting the Masonic Camp
SOURCE: Scottish Rite, Southern Jurisdiction

No single Masonic degree (or similar method of instruction) can teach everything. The royal secret of *equilibrium* reminds us that all of life is itself a balancing act; as much as we strive for improvement or perfection in one area, we must remember there's many other areas or lessons to consider. There's no one Masonic degree that is "better" or "more enlightening" than the rest; the secret of *equilibrium* is that balance must intercede in all things, albeit physical or spiritual. Each degree in Scottish Rite has importance, merit and interrelation amongst the others, otherwise there'd be but a single degree and body, making the degree reunion a half-day affair. The genius of Albert Pike wasn't in his long writing style, but rather his organization and structure of all the Scottish Rite degrees into a single, cohesive philosophy. The degrees are presented in order and in their progression, intentionally; a glance at the apron for this degree (or the *Masonic Camp*) shows this progression symbolically. History is the memory of states [99] and sadly, the continued repetition of mistakes by our human condition. [100]

Pike offers his analysis of *equilibrium*, and, the striving towards perfection due any Prince of the Royal Secret in *Morals and Dogma*. "And this Equilibrium teaches us, above all, to reverence ourselves as immortal souls, and to have respect and charity for others, who are even such as we are, partakers with us of the Divine Nature, lighted by a ray of the Divine Intelligence, struggling, like us, toward the light; capable, like us, of progress upward toward perfection, and deserving to be loved and pitied, but never to be hated nor despised; to be aided and encouraged in this life-struggle, and not to be abandoned nor left to wander in the darkness alone, still less to be trampled upon in our own efforts to ascend." Pike finishes using his own style of tying together the normative concepts from history, along with the spiritual and necessarily empirical physical realms; thus, bringing the integration of balance and *equilibrium*. "—And, finally, of that *Equilibrium*, possible in ourselves, and which Masonry incessantly labors to accomplish in its Initiates, and demands of its Adepts and Princes (else unworthy of their titles), between the Spiritual and Divine and the Material and Human in man; between the Intellect, Reason, and Moral Sense on one side, and the Appetites and Passions on the other, from which result the Harmony and Beauty of a well-regulated life." (Pike, 966)

Pike doesn't view Scottish Rite, or, the Prince of the Royal Secret degree as serving as a blueprint for an ideal civilization or society, but he does end both this degree's chapter and *Morals and Dogma* itself with the passage, "Such my Brother, is the TRUE WORD of a Master Mason; such the true ROYAL SECRET, which makes possible, and shall at length make real, the HOLY EMPIRE of true Masonic Brotherhood." Pike didn't expect average readers to acquire a copy of *Morals and Dogma* when it was published, let alone read it, which may explain many of the semantic nuances in his choice of words and not just in this instance. Pike was careful to not reveal any Masonic secrets with his in-depth dissertations on both the degree's rituals and histories, however, while not a secret book; it wasn't expected (at that period, anyway) to be read by those outside of Scottish Rite. Pike's successor, Grand Commander John Henry Cowles, noted some Masonic books had used large portions of the *Morals and Dogma* text, which he sought to curtail by adding the following words to the title page: "Esoteric Book, for Scottish Rite use only; to be Returned upon Withdrawal or Death of Recipient." [101] Thus, copies of *Morals and Dogma* had this same notice affixed to it for some time. Nonetheless, Pike still envisioned the *Masonic Camp* as a representation of a just and noble society, which might be emulated by others as a good example.

The study of analyzing both past failed civilizations and modern ones has been done at length; the product being that we've evolved quickly in the last 11,000 years (since the discovery of agrarian practices) but they're still integrated with one another in many areas. Thus, the need for careful attention (in both our individual choices and practices, and, those of the state) remains; so, that our society may slowly stop repeating its wrongs and increase instead the correct, ethical approach to solving problems. Consider the following analysis from Jared Diamond: "Of course, much of yesterday's world is still with us today, even in the most densely populated areas of modern industrial societies. Life in sparsely populated rural areas of the Western world still preserves many aspects of traditional societies. Nevertheless, there are big differences between the traditional world and our modern WEIRD (western, educated, industrial, rich and democratic) societies. Traditional peoples have been unconsciously executing thousands of experiments on how to operate a human society. We can't repeat all those experiments intentionally under controlled conditions to see what happens. But we can still learn from what did happen. Some of what yesterday's world teaches us is to be grateful for our modern societies, and not to bad-mouth them across the board. Almost all of us would say good riddance to chronic warfare, infanticide, and abandoning the elderly. We understand why small-scale societies often must do those cruel things, or get trapped into doing them. Fortunately, though, with state governments we're not necessarily trapped in war cycles, and with sedentary lifestyles and food surpluses we're not forced to practice infanticide and abandoning the elderly. We would also say good riddance to the strangling of widows, and to other cruelties that certain traditional societies practice as cultural idiosyncrasies, although nothing about their environment or subsistence forces them to do it." [102]

The seven-pointed star, or heptagram, is revealed for the first time and hangs in the east of the lodge room during the degree ritual. Hutchens explains the symbolism of the Great Symbol in *A Bridge to Light*, "It's a seven-pointed star containing within the points the three lower and four higher colors within a ray of light and visible when the light is passed through a prism. The seven points of this star represent the seven *Amesha Spenta* or "Bountiful Immortals" of the Persian creed, said to have been the source of the emanations of Deity termed by the Kabbalists the *Sephiroth*. Their origin may have been the seven stars of the constellation *Ursa Major,* which naturally divide into the four that form the body and the three that form the tail. Three are female and four are male." (Hutchens, 312)

The observant may take notice that the Great Symbol also resembles the star emblem of the *Order of the Eastern Star*, only with five points instead of seven. The astute notice Pike's assertion that Hiram Abif's murderers' actual names were represented by three stars in a triangle, named Zuben-es Chamali in the West, Zuben-Hak-Rabi in the East, and Zuben-El-Gubi in the South, and, a discussion about the winter solstice. (Pike, 578) More importantly, the theme of integrating historical accounts and the integration of Deity (as well as man's creation) with items of empirical existence, (such as the constellation of *Ursa Major,* or the Lesser and Greater Tetractys) for example, is both continued and reinforced. *Ursa Major* is comprised of seven bright stars; one may theorize they represent the seven noble arts and sciences (or "staircase" as its also known) presented in the symbolic degree of Fellowcraft and then briefly revisited later in the Scottish Rite degree of Knight Kadosh. The companion *Ursa Minor* constellation also contains seven stars, with the brightest star, Polaris, often being the brightest star visible to earth. It's always aligned with the celestial North Pole (making for easy navigation in earlier times) although this will change slightly after some centuries due to the precession of the equinoxes. [103]

"Who before the foundation of this College taught us algebra and arithmetic, astronomy and geometry, chemistry and natural philosophy, and the other mathematical sciences? Who, before her, taught botany, mineralogy, natural history and medical science? To what shall I liken thee, O noble College? To the Star of the East? In that thou art scattering by the rays and mists of the gross darkness of ignorance which has enveloped our native land." [104] One could easily argue the seven liberal arts and sciences are represented by one constellation, with the seven natural sciences representing the other; not unlike Pike's symbolic uses of the Lesser and Greater Tetractys. The seven liberal arts and sciences presented in the Fellowcraft degree are *arithmetic, astronomy, geometry, grammar, logic, music* and *rhetoric*. The seven natural sciences are *astronomy, biology, chemistry, geography, geology, oceanography* and *physics*.

Whilst the "lesser" seven liberal arts and sciences would seem to predate some of the "greater" seven natural sciences, the only which overlaps between both is…astronomy. *Astronomy* teaches the study of the heavens and is the sole intersection between both the "Lesser" and "Greater" disciplines allowing civilization to not only exist, but to peacefully thrive; a central overall theme of both the *Masonic Camp* presented in the thirty-second degree, and, the royal secret of *equilibrium*; its purpose being to keep everything which necessarily exists balanced in harmony.

The science of astronomy tracks the movement of the stars, which reveal that two equinoxes exist per calendar year. The significance of the equinox in Scottish Rite is veiled in allegory, but related to the seven stars in the constellation of *Ursa Minor*. Pike discusses the equinox and its peculiar importance in Scottish Rite most heavily in the Prince of the Tabernacle chapter in *Morals and Dogma* and in the Knight of the Brazen Serpent, with some final mention in the Knight of the Sun, or Prince Adept. No mention of this important link connecting the two brightest constellations in the night sky and the arts and sciences is made in the Prince of the Royal Secret degree, despite its attempt at the unification of the degrees from the four bodies.

Pike used allegory and ancient history to explain much of the important symbolism in Freemasonry, which requires the reader to possess a totality of the work; typically requiring not only participation in Scottish Rite, but intensive personal study as well. Consider De Hoyos' analysis on this important problem: "Beyond social virtues and fraternity, Pike believed that great truths, esoteric and Divine, lay concealed within the symbolism of Freemasonry. This view was partially influenced by his study of early Masonic rituals. For example, in an early ritual of the Sublime Prince of the Royal Secret, it was stated that, "the mysteries of the Craft are the mysteries of religion'" and that the different Masonic degrees were intended to give only "symbolic secrets" to those who could not be trusted with this fact." [105] The casual reader was not prepared to understand the totality of such symbolism and this may explain why contemporary readers (as such) miss many important concepts; this was likely quite intentional. To this point, the origination of Masonic degrees (we learned *previously in the Prince of the Tabernacle degree) originated with the Greater and Lesser Mysteries* of the ancients. Consider the following passage in *Morals and Dogma* concerning this subject.

"At the equinoxes were celebrated the *Greater and Lesser Mysteries of Ceres.* When souls descended past the Balance, at the moment when the Sun occupied that point, the Virgin rose before him; she stood at the gates of day and opened them to him. Her brilliant Star, Spica Virginis, and Arcturus, in Boötes, northwest of it, heralded his coming. When he had returned to the Vernal Equinox, at the moment when souls were generated, again it was the Celestial Virgin that led the march of the signs of night; and in her stars, came the beautiful full moon of that month." (Pike, 606) Later in the Knight of the Brazen Serpent degrees' chapter, Pike returns to this important concept. "The equinoctial year ends at the moment when the Sun and Moon, at the Vernal Equinox, are united with Orion, the Star of Horus, placed in the Heavens under Taurus. The new Moon becomes young again in Taurus, and shows herself as a crescent, for the first time, in the next sign, Gemini, the domicile of Mercury. Then Orion, in conjunction with the Sun, with whom he rises, precipitates the Scorpion, his rival, into the shades of night, causing him to set whenever he himself re-appears on the eastern horizon, with the Sun. Day lengthens and the germs of evil are by degrees eradicated: and Horus (from Aur, Light) reigns triumphant, symbolizing, by his succession to the characteristics of Osiris, the eternal renewal of the Sun's youth and creative vigor at the Vernal Equinox." (Pike, 571)

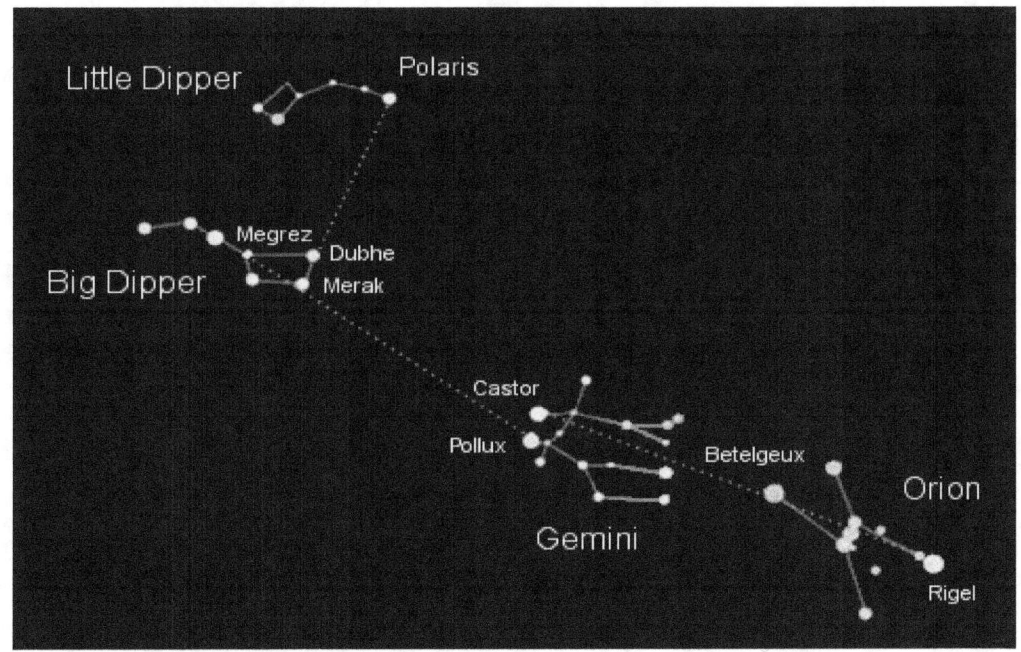

Ursa Major, Minor and Orion at the Vernal Equinox

The overall tracing board of Scottish Rite Freemasonry (if one such existed beyond the Prince of the Royal Secret degree) thus would explain that the *Greater and Lesser mysteries* are not only the true origin of its degrees, but also represent the constellations *Ursa Major* and *Ursa Minor*, which collectively represent the "Lesser" seven liberal arts and sciences and "Greater" seven natural sciences necessary for both the creation and maintenance of an ideal human society. Pike explains this need further: "Every Degree of the *Ancient and Accepted Scottish Rite*, from the first to the thirty-second, teaches by its ceremonial as well as by its instruction, that the noblest purpose of life and the highest duty of a man are to strive incessantly and vigorously to win the mastery of everything, of that which in him is spiritual and divine, over that which is material and sensual; so that in him also, as in the Universe which God governs, *Harmony and Beauty may be the result of a just equilibrium.*" (Pike, 961) This is the true secret lying within the royal secret of *equilibrium*; that balance is necessary not only for the individual's success in life, but also the larger society at-whole. This concept is not just inextricably linked to ancient history and symbolism; it's also presented each night in the sky as a constant reminder to all.

The totality of the Scottish Rite and symbolic "Blue" lodge degrees is a message of civilizing, educating and enlightening the greater society at-large; and not just for Masons themselves. The theme of individual responsibility championing the needs of the deserving and underprivileged is a continued theme observed in the allegory of the degrees, which reinforces the concept of Masonry being a great civilizing tool for society…a shining bright light where otherwise darkness and ignorance would reign. Jean-Baptiste Willermoz, who developed the Rectified Scottish Rite degrees in France and Germany in 1778, described the aims of being a civilizing force in society in *Instruction Secrète des Grands Profès*, while also addressing the allegory and symbolism used so often in its teachings. "Fundamental Masonry, as you have seen, has for itself a single universal aim, something that morality alone cannot fulfill. The practice of moral decency and social responsibility are, it is true, the apparent object of the degrees—but these virtues cannot be their actual aim. What need would she [the Craft] then have for emblems, mysteries and initiation? Her purpose is to enlighten men about his nature, his origin and his destiny." [106]

APPENDIX 1
UNITED STATES SCOTTISH RITE DEGREES

	SOUTHERN JURISDICTION	NORTHERN JURISDICTION
4°	Secret Master	Master Traveler
5°	Perfect Master	Perfect Master
6°	Intimate Secretary	Master of the Brazen Serpent
7°	Provost and Judge	Provost and Judge
8°	Intendant of the Building	Intendant of the Building
9°	Elu of the Nine	Master of the Temple
10°	Elu of the Fifteen	Master Elect
11°	Elu of the Twelve	Sublime Master Elected
12°	Master Architect	Grand Master Architect
13°	Royal Arch of Solomon	Master of the Ninth Arch
14°	Perfect Elu	Grand Elect Mason
15°	Knight of the East	Knight of the East
16°	Prince of Jerusalem	Prince of Jerusalem
17°	Knight of the East and West	Knight of the East and West
18°	Knight Rose Croix	Knight Rose Croix de Heredom
19°	Grand Pontiff	Brother of the Trail
20°	Master of the Symbolic Lodge	Master ad Vitam
21°	Noachite or Prussian Knight	Patriarch Noachite
22°	Knight of the Royal Axe	Prince of Libanus
23°	Chief of the Tabernacle	Chief of the Tabernacle
24°	Prince of the Tabernacle	Brother of the Forest
25°	Knight of the Brazen Serpent	Master of Achievement
26°	Prince of Mercy	Friend and Brother Eternal
27°	Knight of the Sun	Knight of Jerusalem
28°	Knight Cmdr. of the Temple	Knight of the Sun
29°	Scottish Knight of St. Andrew	Knight of Saint Andrew
30°	Knight Kadosh	Grand Inspector
31°	Inspector Inquisitor	Knight Aspirant
32°	Master of the Royal Secret	Sublime Prince of the Royal Secret

APPENDIX II
STATES IN EACH U.S. JURISDICTION

NORTHERN JURISDICTION	SOUTHERN JURISDICTION
Connecticut	Alabama
Delaware	Alaska
Illinois	Arizona
Indiana	Arkansas
Maine	California
Massachusetts	Colorado
Michigan	Florida
New Jersey	Georgia
New Hampshire	Hawaii
New York	Idaho
Ohio	Iowa
Pennsylvania	Kansas
Rhode Island	Kentucky
Wisconsin	Louisiana
Vermont	Maryland
	Minnesota
	Mississippi
	Montana
	Nebraska
	Nevada
	New Mexico
	North Carolina
	North Dakota
	Oklahoma
	Oregon
	South Carolina
	South Dakota
	Tennessee
	Texas
	Utah
	Virginia
	Washington
	West Virginia
	Wyoming

APPENDIX III
SCOTTISH RITE DEGREES IN AUSTRALIA & CANADA

	AUSTRALIA	CANADA
4°	Secret Master	Secret Master
5°	Perfect Master	Perfect Master
6°	Intimate Secretary	Intimate Secretary
7°	Provost and Judge	Provost and Judge
8°	Intendant of the Building	Intendant of the Building
9°	Elu of the Nine	Elu of the Nine
10°	Elu of the Fifteen	Elu of the Fifteen
11°	Elu of the Twelve	Elu of the Twelve
12°	Master Architect	Grand Master Architect
13°	Royal Arch of Enoch	Royal Arch of Solomon
14°	Grand Elect Perfect & Sublime Mason	Grand Elect Perfect & S.Mason
15°	Knight of the East	Knight of the East
16°	Prince of Jerusalem	Prince of Jerusalem
17°	Knight of the East and West	Knight of the East and West
18°	Prince Rose Croix of Heredom	Knight Rose Croix
19°	Grand Pontiff	Grand Pontiff
20°	Master of the Symbolic Lodge	Master ad Vitam
21°	Noachite or Prussian Knight	Patriarch Noachite
22°	Knight of the Royal Axe	Prince of Libanus
23°	Chief of the Tabernacle	Chief of the Tabernacle
24°	Prince of the Tabernacle	Prince of the Tabernacle
25°	Knight of the Brazen Serpent	Knight of the Brazen Serpent
26°	Prince of Mercy	Prince of Mercy
27°	Knight of the Sun	Commander of the Temple
28°	Knight Cmdr. of the Temple	Knight of the Sun
29°	Scottish Knight of St. Andrew	Knight of Saint Andrew
30°	Grand Elect Knight Kadosh	Knight Kadosh
31°	Grand Inspector Inquisitor Cmdr.	Inspector Inquisitor Commander
32°	Sublime Prince of the Royal Secret	Sublime Prince of Royal Secret

APPENDIX IV
FUNDAMENTAL DEGREES OF FREEMASONRY

1°	Entered Apprentice
2°	Fellowcraft
3°	Master Mason
4°	Secret Master
14°	Perfect Elu
16°	Prince of Jerusalem
18°	Knight Rose Croix
30°	Knight Kadosh

RECOMMENDED DEGREE REUNION ADDITIONS

13°	Royal Arch of Solomon
15°	Knight of the East
23°	Chief of the Tabernacle
25°	Knight of the Brazen Serpent
29°	Scottish Knight of St. Andrew

FEAST OF TISHRI (or FEAST OF THE TABERNACLE)

1866 *Statutes of Supreme Council* select September 15.
1885 Revising Committee select December 27.
1886 Pike declares September 15th the *Feast Day of Perfect Elu's.*
1905 *Laws and Statutes* using September 15 is published.

AGENDA FOR OBSERVANCE

1. Open *Lodge of Perfect Elu's* in full, or short form.

2. Reading of "Why the Feast of Tishri?"

3. Reading of the *Fourteenth-Degree obligation.*

4. The brethren shall then join in prayer.

5. The *Lodge of Perfect Elu's* is closed in full or short form.

6. The brethren shall retire and join their guests for the feast.

7. Observance toasts made standing with grape juice or red wine.

APPENDIX VI
WHY THE FEAST OF TISHRI?

The origins and significances of the *feast of Tishri* make it the most Scottish Rite of festivals. Although originally celebrated as a harvest and gathering festival, no other occasion epitomizes the character and purpose of the Rite more wholly than our historic celebration, held in conjunction with the dedication of King Solomon's Temple (*2 Chronicles 7:8-10*). To marshal the meanings of the feast are to summarize the principal ideals and traditions of our Fraternity.

First, we observe the *feast of Tishri* because it is an ancient custom. Under the *Statutes of the Supreme Council*, the feast was considered an obligatory observance, a sharing of our fraternal spirit. Freemasons have always revered order since we recognize that there is a Supreme Order that structures all creation. Masonic Law emulates this divine order, and we serve the purposes of the Great Architect of the Universe and we meet in the bonds of brotherhood; intent on making contributions to humanity.

Secondly, the rich legendry of the Temple's dedication (held along with the *feast of Tishri*) is an essential part of the Fourteenth Degree. The symbolic details of the Temples position, design, construction, furnishing, and decoration carries special meaning as they apply to the metaphysical Temple of Freemasonry built in the heart of every brother. Through the symbols of the Temple, we learn to recommit ourselves to building Freemasonry "in the hearts of men and among nations."

Significantly, Solomon, A king of peace and wisdom, built the Temple. The Lord forbade David, a warrior and a man of blood, to construct the Temple and, instead, delivered this responsibility and glory to Solomon, whose very name derives from the Hebrew word *shalom*, meeting peace. Thus, in observing the *feast of Tishri*, we reaffirm our dedication to human concord and the brotherhood of all men in a world of peace. As individuals and as brothers in the Rite, we resolved to build, as Solomon did, through harmony and cooperation, ever seeking peace for all mankind.

The consecration of the Temple must also be observed at the *feast of Tishri* because it teaches the equality in unity of all members of the Rite. The people of Israel, unified under Solomon, were equal in their devotion to the Lord and equal in their sovereignty to all other nations. In the *feast of Tishri*, all Perfect Elu's and those of higher degrees can join at the banquet table and share in the bond of fraternal unity.

Yet another reason to keep the *feast of Tishri* is that such observance fosters the warm spirit of fraternal fellowship so vital to the Rite. We meet at a common table, express our mutual esteem, and so promote that essential bond of cordiality and respect which lightens and shares the way of our Masonic endeavors. Such social amenities open us to each other in an atmosphere elevated beyond the sphere of normal, day-to-day communication. Within the context of the *feast of Tishri*, we realize more deeply than ever before the value of our fellowmen, without which the individual is lost in a self-imposed prison of human isolation.

Lastly, the *law, legendry, peace, equality, unity,* and *fellowship* of the *feast of Tishri* combine to make this most Masonic feast of feasts. At the reflection table, all--Jew, Christian, Muslim, Buddhist, and others--join a common voice of thanksgiving where every man can share his gratitude and express his sincere thanks to Him, who made all things. The deity has given us life, the strength to live it fully, and the joy of sharing the beauty and goodness of His creation with our fellowmen. Most of all, He has given us freedom. The *feast of Tishri* celebrates this freedom which the Israelites one with the guidance of Providence, despite the shackles of Egypt and the armies of the Philistines.

The ancient victory celebrated in the dedication of Solomon's Temple is kept forever fresh through our keeping of the *feast of Tishri*. It promises to all men that the burdens of tyranny are temporary, that the darkness will yield to light, that knowledge will conquer ignorance, and that the Creator intended men to be free. The message of *Tishri* comes to us strongly and clearly from across the ages because it has been so preserved in the symbolism and allegory of the Scottish Rite. Through our observance of this great feast of thanksgiving, we, as heirs of Solomon, perpetuate his magnificent temple of freedom in our lives, our communities, our country and, most of all, in our beloved Rite.

SOURCE: *Forms and Traditions of the Scottish* Rite
C. Fred Kleinknecht, 33°

ACKNOWLEDGMENTS

I'd like to thank my wife Susan; for her support and love during the writing of this book, and, in general.

I'd next like to thank Rex Hutchens for writing *A Bridge to Light*. This is the first text I recommend for those who enjoyed this book and want to learn more about the degrees. It's affordable, concise and easy to read.

Many thanks go to the Grand Archivist & Historian of Scottish Rite, Arturo De Hoyos, who's authored many superb books, including *The Scottish Rite Ritual Monitor & Guide*. This hefty "doorstop" is invaluable and recommended as the next read for the curious.

Lastly, I must thank the late Albert Pike for his reorganization and rewriting of these degrees, as well as for writing *Morals and Dogma*. De Hoyos' annotated version's the first that's truly readable for modern audiences; it should be read next and is an excellent investment.

ABOUT THE AUTHOR

Darren completed undergraduate and graduate degree programs in political science at *California State University, Fullerton.*

He lives in Silicon Valley and works as a technologist and writer.

The author's a fourth generation Freemason, a member of *The Philalethes Society*, and, *The Grand College of Rites.* He was conferred a *Baron of the German Nation* by the *Order of Teutonic Knights* in 2014 and is active in his community.

REFERENCES

[1] Portal, Frédéric. *An Essay on Symbolic Colours: In Antiquity--The Middle Ages—And Modern Times.* J. Weale. 1845. (6)

[2] Gage, John. *Color and Meaning: Art, Science and Symbolism.* University of California Press. 1999. (109)

[3] McClenachan, Charles, Thompson. *The Book of the Ancient and Accepted Scottish Rite of Freemasonry: Containing Instructions on All the Degrees from the Third to the Thirty-third and Last Degree of the Rite; Together with Ceremonies on Inauguration, Institution, Grand Visitations, Refections, Lodges of Sorrow, Adoption, Constitutions, General Regulations, Calendar, Etc.* Masonic Publications & Manufacturing. 1868. (26)

[4] Pike, Albert. *Morals and Dogma: Of the Ancient and Accepted Scottish Rite of Freemasonry: Annotated Edition.* Supreme Council. 2011. (193)

[5] Arturo De Hoyos. *The Scottish Rite Ritual Monitor and Guide.* Supreme Council, 33°, Ancient and Accepted Scottish Rite of Freemasonry, Southern Jurisdiction, U.S.A. (157)

[6] Rex Hutchens. *A Bridge to Light.* Supreme Council, 33°, Ancient and Accepted Scottish Rite of Freemasonry, Southern Jurisdiction, U.S.A., 1995. (40)

[7] Samuel Freeman. Edward N. Zalta (ed.) *"Original Position", The Stanford Encyclopedia of Philosophy (Spring 2012 Edition).* Stanford University Press. 2012.

[8] Thomas Jackson. *Masonic Education: Looking to the Future,* Conference of Grand Secretaries of North America, 2012. (40)

[9] John Rawls. *A Theory of Justice (Revised Edition).* Harvard University Press. 2009. (11)

[10] Rhode Island Scottish Rite – *Valley of Providence.* http://www.riscottishrite.org

[11] University of Bradford – *Web of Hiram, Degrees of the Ancient & Accepted Scottish Rite.*
http://www.brad.ac.uk/webofhiram/?section=ancient_accepted&page=8Intendant.html

[12] Nozick, Robert. *Philosophical Explanations.* Harvard University Press. 1981. (366)

[13] *Book of Deuteronomy* 19:17-21.

[14] *Book of Exodus* 21:23-21.

[15] Martin, Jacqueline. *The English Legal System* (4th ed.) 2005. (174)

[16] Rachels, James. *The Elements of Moral Philosophy.* McGraw-Hill Education. 2007.

[17] *Turner, Ralph v. Magna Carta Pearson.* 2003. (210)

[18] Mackey, Albert. *The Principles of Masonic Law: A Treatise on the Constitutional Laws, Usages and Landmarks of Freemasonry.* 1856.

[19] Moreno, Barry. *The Statue of Liberty Encyclopedia.* Schuster. 2000.

[20] The Builder, February 1915, *The Fourth Degree*
http://www.masonicdictionary.com/feb1915g.html

[21] BBC web feature on July 21, 2012.

[22] Num. 19 and Babylonian Talmud, Tractate *Chagigah.* (12)

[23] Barnes, Albert. *Barnes' Notes on the New Testament.* Kregel Publications. 1962. Matthew 3:6.

[24] *Encyclopedia of Freemasonry.*
http://encyclopediaofFreemasonry.com/l/lustration/

[25] Tollington, Janet, E. *Tradition and Innovation in Haggai and Zechariah 1-8.* A&C Black. 1993. (132)

[26] Russell, Edgar, A. *Thoughts Inspired by the A.A. Scottish Rite Degrees*. E.A. Russell Company. 1919. (85)

[27] Epstein, Marc, Michael. *Dreams of Subversion in Medieval Jewish Art and Literature*. Penn State Press. 1997. (110)

[28] Floyd, Michael and Haak, Robert, D. *Prophets, Prophecy, and Prophetic Texts in the Second Temple Judaism*. A&C Black. 2006. (104)

[29] *Book of Ezra* 6:3–5.

[30] *Book of Chronicles* 36:23-2.

[31] Becker, Udo. *The Continuum of Symbols*. A&C Black. 2000. (133)

[32] *Book of Nehemiah* 4:14-20.

[33] *Book of Ezra* 5:1-2.

[34] *1 Timothy 2. First Epistle of Paul to Timothy. New Testament.*

[35] Stuckenbrook. Loren, T. *Commentaries on Early Jewish Literature*. De Gruyter. 2003. (1536)

[36] Mounce, Robert, H. *The Book of Revelation (The New International Commentary on the New Testament)*. Wm. B. Eerdmans Publishing Company. 1998. (32)

[37] Paton, Chalmers, Izett. *Freemasonry: Its Symbolism, Religious Nature, and Law of Perfection*. Reeves and Turner. 1873. (110)

[38] *Romans 1:23. The Epistle to the Romans. New Testament.*

[39] Karris, Robert, J. *The Collegeville Bible Commentary: New Testament*. Liturgical Press. 1992. (1296)

[40] Yanker, John. *The Arcane Schools (Extended Illustrated & Annotated Edition)*. Jazzybee Verlag. 2013. (576)

[41] McIntosh, Christopher. *The Rosicrucian's: The History, Mythology and Rituals of an Esoteric Order.* Weiser Books. 1998. (xiii)

[42] Clymer, Swinburne, R. *Rose Cross Order: History Repeats Itself.* Health Research Books. 1996. (198)

[43] Mackey, Albert. *An Encyclopedia of Masonry and its Kindred Sciences: Comprising the Whole Range of the Arts, Sciences and Literature as Connected with the Institution, Volume 2.* Masonic History Company. 1920. (638)

[44] Picart, Bernard. *Histoire des Religions et des Moeurs de Tous les Peuples du Monde.* Nicolle. 1819. (152)

[45] Waite, Arthur, Edward. *The Secret Tradition in Freemasonry and an Analysis of the Inter-Relation Between the Craft and the High Grades in Respect of Their Term of Research, Expressed by the way of Symbolism.* Rebman Limited. 1911. (401)

[46] Lewis Spencer, H. *Complete History of the Rosicrucian Order.* Book Tree. 2006. (174)

[47] Jenkins, Phillip. *Cults and New Religions in American History.* Oxford University Press. 2000. (74)

[48] Melton, Gordon, J. *The Encyclopedia of American Religions, Religious Creeds: A Compilation of More than 450 Creeds, Confessions, Statements of Faith, and Summaries of Doctrine of Religious and Spiritual Groups in the United States and Canada.* Gale Research Company. 1988. (179)

[49] Gilbert, A.R. *The Masonic Career of A.E. Waite.* Transactions of Quatuor Coronati Lodge #2076. 1986.

[50] United States Foreign Intelligence Surveillance Court. http://www.fisc.uscourts.gov

[51] Assmann, Jan, *The Search for God in Ancient Egypt.* Cornell University Press. 2001. (80)

[52] Miroslav, Marcovich, ed., *Refutatio Omnium Haeresium*, Walter de Gruyter, 1986.

[53] Smith, William. *A Dictionary of Greek and Roman Antiquities*. London, 1875.

[54] Cline, Eric and O'Connor, David. *Thutmose III: A New Biography*. University of Michigan Press. 2006. (127)

[55] Curl, James Stevens. *The Egyptian Revival: Ancient Egypt as the Inspiration for Design Motifs in the West*. Routledge. 2013. (231)

[56] Atkinson, William Walter. *Reincarnation and the Law of Karma / A Study of the Old-New World-Doctrine of Rebirth, and Spiritual Cause and Effect*. Yogi Publication Society. 1908. (20)

[57] Bement, R.B. *Tyre: The History of Phoenicia, Palestine and Syria, and the Final Captivity of Israel and Judah by the Assyrians*. Ulan Press. 2012. (47)

[58] Morris, Robert. *Freemasonry in the Holy Land, Or, Landmarks of Hiram's Builders: Embracing Notes Made During a Series of Masonic Researches, in 1868, in Asia Minor, Syria, Palestine, Egypt, and Europe, and the Correspondence with Freemasons in Those Countries*. Palestine. 1877. (46)

[59] Gershom, Yonasson. *Jewish Tales of Reincarnation*. Jason Aronson, Incorporated. 2000. (20)

[60] Fellows, John. *The Mysteries of Freemasonry*. Рипол Классик. 1860. (94)

[61] World of Tasawwuf.
http://www.spiritualfoundation.net/fatherofsufism.htm

[62] Kayum, Sajid Abdul. *The Jamaat Tableegh and the Deobandis*. AHYA Multi-Media. 2001.

[63] Zaruq, Ahmed. Istrabadi, Zaineb. Hanson, Hanza Yusuf. *The Principles of Sufism.* Amal Press. 2008.

[64] Lewis, Richard Farnell. *Greek Hero Cults and Ideas of Immortality.* Kessinger Publishing. 2004. (234)

[65] Lock, Stephen. Last, John and Dunea, George. *The Oxford Illustrated Companion to Medicine.* Oxford University Press. 2001. (261)

[66] Schouten, Jan. *The Rod and Serpent of Asclepius: Symbol of Medicine.* Elsevier Publishing Company. 1967. (2)

[67] Edelstein, Emma and Ludwig. *Asclepius: Collection and Interpretation of the Testimonies.* Johns Hopkins University Press. 1998. (13)

[68] Allman, George. *Greek Geometry from Thales to Euclid.* Hodges, Figgis and Co. 1889. (183)

[69] Child, Heather & Colles, Dorothy. *Christian Symbols, Ancient and Modern: A Handbook for Students.* Scribner. 1972.

[70] Morgan, Gerald. *The Significance of the Pentangle Symbolism in "Sir Gawain and the Green Knight."* The Modern Language Review. 1979. (769)

[71] Nicolle, David. *Teutonic Knight: 1190-1561.* Osprey Publishing. 2007.

[72] *The Teutonic Knights of St. Mary's Hospital in Jerusalem* Deutscher Orden
http://www.imperialteutonicorder.com/index.html

[73] Felltham, Owen. *Resolves Divine – Moral - Political.* London: Whittaker & Co., 1840. (121)

[74] Millington, Ellen. *Heraldry in History.* London: Chapman and Hall. 1858. (78)

[75] Elliot, J.K. editor. *The Apocryphal New Testament: A Collection of Apocryphal Christian Literature in an English Translation.* Oxford University Press. 1963. (369)

[76] Dvornick, Francis. *The Idea of Apostolicity in Byzantium and the Legend of the Apostle Andrew.* Literary Licensing, LLC. 2011.

[77] Calvert, Judith. *The Iconography of the St. Andrew Auckland Cross.* The Art Bulletin, December 1984. (543)

[78] Langdon, Helen. *Caravaggio: A Life.* Westview Press. 2000.

[79] Mackey, Albert. *An Encyclopedia of Freemasonry and its Kindred Sciences, Comprising the Whole Range of Arts, Sciences and Literature as Connected with the Institution, Volume 2.* Masonic History Company. 1912. (658)

[80] Hanson, Levett Sir. *An Accurate Historical Account of all the Orders of Knighthood at Present Existing in Europe, by an Officer of the Chancery of the Equestrian Order of Saint Joachim.* Oxford University. 1802. (15)

[81] Nisbet, Alexander. *A System of Heraldry, Speculative and Practical, With the True art of Blazon, according to the Most Approved Heralds in Europe: Illustrated With ... and Genealogical Memorials Relative Thereto.* J. Mack Euen. 1722. (125)

[82] Clark, Hugh. *A Concise History of Knighthood, Volume 1.* London. 1784. (123)

[83] Zitser, Ernest. *The Transfigured Kingdom: Sacred Parody and Charismatic Authority at the Court of Peter the Great.* Cornell University Press. 2004. (90)

[84] Boulton Dacre, D'Arcy Jonathan. *The Knights of the Crown: The Monarchial Orders of Knighthood in Later Medieval Europe, 1325-1520.* Boydell Press. 2000. (17)

[85] Korb, Johann Georg. *Diary of an Austrian Secretary of Legation at the Court of Czar Peter the Great, Volume 1*. HardPress Publishing. 2012. (272)

[86] Pike, Albert. *Knight Kadosh Degree*. Kessinger Publishing. 2010.

[87] Hotema, Hilton. *Pre-Existence of Man*. Health Research Books. 1998. (10)

[88] Ancient & Accepted Scottish Rite of Freemasonry, S.J., USA. *Statutes of The Supreme Council of the Thirty-Third Degree*. 2011. (21)

[89] Pike, Albert. *Officers of Constitution and Inauguration of a Council of Knights Kadosh*. 1879. (19)

[90] Chaplin, W.J., editor. *Michigan Freemason: A Monthly Magazine Devoted to Masonic and Home Literature, Volume VIII*. Ihling Brothers, Publishers and Proprietors. 1877. (386)

[91] Nicholson, Helen. Reynolds, Wayne. *Knight Templar 1120-1312*. Osprey Publishing. 2004. (24)

[92] Taylor, John, H. *Journey Through the Afterlife: Ancient Egyptian Book of the Dead*. Harvard University Press. 2010. (55)

[93] Allen, James, P. *Middle Egyptian: An Introduction to the Language and Culture of Hieroglyphs*. Cambridge University Press. 2000. (316)

[94] Budge, Wallis, E.A. *The Book of the Dead: The Hieroglyphic Transcript and Translation into English of the Papyrus of Ani*. Gramercy Books. 1995. (576)

[95] Faulkner, Raymond, O. *The Ancient Egyptian Book of the Dead*. University of Texas Press. 1990. (14)

[96] Pinch, Geraldine. *Magic in Ancient Egypt*. University of Texas Press. 1995. (155)

[97] De Motte, Earle. *Egyptian Religion and Mysteries*. Xlibris Corporation. 2013. (46)

[98] Strauss Leo. *"Natural Law" in…International Encyclopedia of the Social Sciences*. Macmillan. 1968.

[99] Kissinger, Henry. *A World Restored: Metternich, Castlereagh and the Problems of Peace, 1812-22 (Weidenfeld & Nicolson 50 Years)*. Odyssey Editions. 2013. (10)

[100] Horowitz, Irving, L. *The Decomposition of Sociology*. Oxford University Press. 1993. (228)

[101] *Transactions of the Supreme Council, 33°, Southern Jurisdiction*. House of the Temple. 1947. (38)

[102] Diamond, Jared. *The World Until Yesterday: What Can We Learn from Traditional Societies?* Viking Adult. 2012. (461)

[103] Guilherme de Almeida. *Navigating the Night Sky: How to Identify the Stars and Constellations*. Springer London. 2004.

[104] Morris, Robert. *Freemasonry in the Holy Land; Or, Landmarks of Hiram's Builders; Embracing Notes Made During a Series of Masonic Researches, in 1868, in Asia Minor, Syria, Palestine, Egypt and Europe, and the Results of Much Correspondence with Freemasons in Those Countries*. 1873. (237)

[105] Pike, Albert. *Albert Pike's Esoterica: The Symbolism of the Blue Degrees of Freemasonry*. Scottish Rite Research Society. 2005. (xxv)

[106] Du Pays de l'Ours, Celui. *Entre le Cygne et l'Ours. Le Centre Sacré des Gaules*. LuLu.com. 2012. (17)